D0139269

ManageFirst®
Food Production
Competency Guide

Donated by
◈ Chef Michael Therriat ◈

PEARSON
Prentice
Hall

Upper Saddle River, New Jersey 07458

NATIONAL
RESTAURANT
ASSOCIATION
SOLUTIONS ™

Disciaimer

Table of Contents

A Message from the National Restaurant Association

Founded in 1919, the National Restaurant Association is the leading business association for the restaurant industry. Together with the National Restaurant Association Educational Foundation (NRAEF) and National Restaurant Association Solutions (NRA Solutions) our goal is to lead America's restaurant industry into a new era of prosperity, prominence, and participation, enhancing the quality of life for all we serve.

As one of the nation's largest private-sector employers, the restaurant, hospitality and foodservice industry is the cornerstone of the American economy, of career-and-employment opportunities, and of local communities. The overall impact of the restaurant industry is astounding. The restaurant industry is expected to add 1.8 million jobs over the next decade, with employment reaching 14.8 million by 2019. At the National Restaurant Association, we are focused on enhancing this position by providing the valuable tools and resources needed to educate our current and future professionals.

For more information on the National Restaurant Association, please visit our Web site at www.restaurant.org.

What is the ManageFirst Program™?

The ManageFirst Program is a management-training certificate program that exemplifies our commitment to developing materials by the industry, for the industry. The program's most powerful strength is that it is based on a set of competencies defined by the restaurant, foodservice, and hospitality industry as critical for success. For more information on the ManageFirst Program, visit www.managefirst.restaurant.org.

ManageFirst Program Components

The ManageFirst Program includes a set of Competency Guides, exams, Instructor Resources, certificates, a credential, and support activities and services. By participating in the program, you are demonstrating your commitment to becoming a highly qualified professional either preparing to begin or to advance your career in the restaurant, hospitality, and foodservice industry.

The Competency Guides cover the range of topics listed in the chart at right.

Competency Guide/Exam Topics

ManageFirst Core Credential Topics

Controlling Foodservice Costs

Hospitality and Restaurant Management

Human Resources Management and Supervision

ServSafe® Food Safety

ManageFirst Elective Topics

Customer Service

Food Production

Inventory and Purchasing

Managerial Accounting

Menu Marketing and Management

Nutrition

Restaurant Marketing

ServSafe Alcohol® Responsible Alcohol Service

Within the guides, you will find the essential content for the topic as defined by industry, as well as learning activities, assessments, case studies, suggested field projects, professional profiles, and testimonials. You can also find an answer sheet or an online exam voucher for a NRA Solutions exam written specifically for each topic. The exam can be administered either online or in a paper and pencil format (see inside front cover for a listing of ISBNs), and it will be proctored. Upon successfully passing the exam, you will be issued a customized certificate from NRA Solutions. The certificate is a lasting recognition of your accomplishment and a signal to the industry that you have mastered the competency covered within the particular topic.

To earn the ManageFirst Professional™ (MFP™) credential, you will be required to pass four core exams and one elective exam (to be chosen from the remaining program topics) and to document your work experience in the restaurant and foodservice industry. Earning the MFP credential is a significant accomplishment.

We applaud you as you either begin or advance your career in the restaurant, hospitality, and foodservice industry. Visit *www.managefirst.restaurant.org* to learn about additional career-building resources offered through the National Restaurant Association, including scholarships for college students enrolled in relevant industry programs.

ManageFirst Program Ordering Information

Review copies or support materials:
FACULTY FIELD SERVICES
Tel: 800.526.0485

Domestic orders and inquiries:
PEARSON CUSTOMER SERVICE
Tel: 800.922.0579
www.prenhall.com

International orders and inquiries:
U.S. EXPORT SALES OFFICE
Pearson Education International Customer Service Group
200 Old Tappan Road
Old Tappan, NJ 07675 USA
Tel: 201.767.5021
Fax: 201.767.5625

**For corporate, government and special sales
(consultants, corporations, training centers, VARs, and
corporate resellers) orders and inquiries:**
PEARSON CORPORATE SALES
Tel: 317.428.3411
Fax: 317.428.3343
Email: managefirst@prenhall.com

For additional information regarding other Prentice Hall
publications, instructor and student support materials,
locating your sales representative and much more,
please visit *www.prenhall.com/managefirst.*

Acknowledgements

The National Restaurant Association Solutions is grateful for the significant contributions made to this competency guide by the following individuals.

Thomas C. Kaltenecker, CHE, MCFE

In addition, we are pleased to thank our many other advisors, subject matter experts, reviewers, and contributors for their time, effort, and dedication to this program.

Teresa Marie Gargano Adamski	**John Hart**	**James Perry**
Ernest Boger	**Ray Kavanaugh**	**Patricia Plavcan**
Robert Bosselman	**John Kidwell**	**William N. Reynolds**
Jerald Chesser	**Carol Kizer**	**Rosenthal Group**
Cynthia Deale	**Holly Ruttan Maloney**	**Mokie Steiskal**
Fred DeMicco	**Cynthia Mayo**	**Karl Titz**
Johnathan Deustch	**Fred Mayo**	**Terry Umbreit**
John Drysdale	**Patrick Moreo**	**David R. Wightman**
Gene Fritz	**Robert O'Halloran**	**Deanne Williams**
John Gescheidle	**Brian O'Malley**	**Mike Zema**
Thomas Hamilton	**Terrence Pappas**	**Renee Zonka**

Features of the ManageFirst® Competency Guides

We have designed the ManageFirst competency guides to enhance your ability to learn and retain important information that is critical to this restaurant and foodservice industry function. Here are the key features you will find within this guide.

Beginning Each Guide

Tuning In to You

When you open a ManageFirst competency guide for the first time, you might ask yourself: Why do I need to know about this topic? Every topic of these guides involves key information you will need as you manage a restaurant or foodservice operation. Located in the front of each review guide, "Tuning In to You" is a brief synopsis that illustrates some of the reasons the information contained throughout that particular guide is important to you. It exemplifies real-life scenarios that you will face as a manager and how the concepts in the book will help you in your career.

Professional Profile

This is your opportunity to meet a professional who is currently working in the field associated with a competency guide's topic. This person's story will help you gain insight into the responsibilities related to his or her position, as well as the training and educational history linked to it. You will also see the daily and cumulative impact this position has on an operation, and receive advice from a person who has successfully met the challenges of being a manager.

Beginning Each Chapter

Inside This Chapter

Chapter content is organized under these major headings.

Learning Objectives

Learning objectives identify what you should be able to do after completing each chapter. These objectives are linked to the required tasks a manager must be able to perform in relation to the function discussed in the competency guide.

Test Your Knowledge

Each chapter begins with some True or False questions designed to test your prior knowledge of some of the concepts presented in the chapter. The answers to these questions, as well as the concepts behind them, can be found within the chapter—see the page reference after each question.

Key Terms

These terms are important for thorough understanding of the chapter's content. They are highlighted throughout the chapter, where they are explicitly defined or their meaning is made clear within the paragraphs in which they appear.

Throughout Each Chapter

Exhibits

Exhibits are placed throughout each chapter to visually reinforce the key concepts presented in the text. Types of exhibits include charts, tables, photographs, and illustrations.

Think About It...

These thought-provoking sidebars reveal supportive information about the section they appear beside.

Activities

Apply what you have learned throughout the chapter by completing the various activities in the text. The activities have been designed to give you additional practice and better understanding of the concepts addressed in the learning objectives. Types of activities include case studies, role-plays, and problem solving, among others.

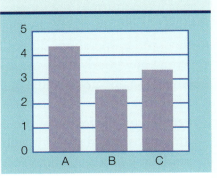

Exhibit

Exhibits are visuals that will help you learn about key concepts.

Think About It...

Consider these supplemental insights as you read through a chapter.

Activity

Activity

Types of activities you will complete include case studies, role-plays, and problem solving, among others.

At the End of Each Chapter

Review Your Learning

These multiple-choice or open- or close-ended questions or problems are designed to test your knowledge of the concepts presented in the chapter. These questions have been aligned with the objectives and should provide you with an opportunity to practice or apply the content that supports these objectives. If you have difficulty answering them, you should review the content further.

At the End of the Guide

Field Project

This real-world project gives you the valuable opportunity to apply many of the concepts you will learn in a competency guide. You will interact with industry practitioners, enhance your knowledge, and research, apply, analyze, evaluate, and report on your findings. It will provide you with an in-depth "reality check" of the policies and practices of this management function.

Tuning In to You

Experimenting in the kitchen can produce some fantastic results—or some dreadful ones. Who hasn't discovered an unlikely combination that tastes terrific? Likewise, who hasn't added just a pinch too much of a spice and ruined a dish? While someone cooking at home might laugh off a mistake, restaurant and foodservice operations do not have that luxury. An experiment gone wrong or a poorly prepared dish turns into a dissatisfied customer, which usually means a loss of sales. Likewise, when a menu item is extremely popular, an operation must be able to meet its customers' demand for the item and provide the same wonderful dish every time it is ordered or risk turning people away. Too many problems producing quality food and an operation may find itself in serious jeopardy of closing. That is why successful operations rely on documented processes for consistently preparing and presenting menu items, delivering the same high-quality dishes to customers day after day.

As the manager of an operation, you will be responsible for the quality of the menu items your employees serve. You must understand the processes an operation needs for quality food production, know how to establish these processes, and ensure your staff is following them, from purchasing and receiving to cooking and service.

A particular challenge to quality food production is high-volume situations. If you work in or plan to pursue a career in catering, banquet services, or other large-scale events, you will have special considerations for ensuring quality. Every guest of a 450-person event expects the exact same quality of food at the exact same time. Coordinating the preparation and service and working out the logistics of an off-site event takes even more attention to the standards and procedures you have established. You must also consider what to do with the inevitable leftovers: can they safely be used again without diminishing the quality of your dishes?

Whether serving fifty people in one night or in one sitting, you will realize as you manage an operation that implementing quality in food production is an ongoing process. Since there are many components to a good meal—the right ingredients, proper preparation and cooking, excellent service—it is a challenge to keep quality at top level at all times. The system of standards, policies, and procedures you put in place will go a long way in ensuring that quality is a concern for all your employees. This system, if monitored and revised as your operation changes and grows, will reveal itself to your customers in only the best of ways: superb menu items every time.

Professional Profile
Your opportunity to meet someone working in the field

Michael Shoemaker

Proprietor
Noteable Event Productions
Lombard, IL

I started my career in the restaurant and foodservice industry by helping in a friend's restaurant in a rural Wisconsin town, from junior high through high school. I was pretty sure that I wanted to stay in the industry, but I took a break to see whether I'd like another field. After one week working in a foundry, I decided to return to restaurants. After high school, I gained experience in other aspects of the foodservice industry by working at a Holiday Inn. I welcomed the bigger setting, challenge, and variety. With encouragement from a mentor, I completed an associate degree from the Milwaukee Area Technical College.

With my degree in hand, I moved to Oak Brook, Illinois, a suburb west of Chicago, and stayed with a friend while we worked in a hotel chain—day and night. But I learned a lot. At that time, headquarters of large corporations were changing their in-house foodservices from fairly bland offerings to a variety of food, including ethnic and healthy options. I was asked to join a Chicago-area corporation, Motorola, to lead this change.

The changed menu was so successful that our in-house foodservice team began catering in-house events, from department functions to events that the company sponsored for the public, such as the Western Open Golf Tournament. It became a profit center.

After twenty years, Motorola began shifting again. The corporation reevaluated its core businesses, and, although the foodservice unit was profitable, it wasn't a part of the core business. I knew that I would need to make another change. I talked with some associates and friends about the idea starting my own catering business. Everyone encouraged me, so I decided to take the plunge.

The new business was started in a building of twenty-five hundred square feet in 1998. I bought used equipment, got permits from the health department, and installed two telephone lines. Eighteen months later, Noteable Event Productions had outgrown that space.

I took a bigger plunge and leased a space in the main floor of a corporate office building. In addition to continuing to grow the catering business, I wanted to get as much revenue from the space as possible. I opened a forty-foot-long café for the people who worked in the building. Over the last five years, I have added four more cafés in the suburbs. On weekends, the staff gives cooking demonstrations in the building. The demos provide exposure to the business as well as additional income. After Motorola got out of the catering business, local golf tournament staff put out a bid for the two golf tournaments held each year in our area. Noteable Event Productions won the bid in 2003 for the large events.

Summers are the busiest times, with many tenant appreciation events ranging from ice cream socials to full banquet dinners. Decembers are also filled with corporate and social events.

Advertising is all word of mouth. When anyone shows an interest in using Noteable Events, I send one of three sales persons to visit the potential client. The sales person brings our signature, chocolate-dipped cookies to the meeting. The only other advertising expenses are the Web site and a three-fold brochure.

A surprising benefit of my business, after working years for others, is that I see my family more now. My family—wife and children—are able to help in the business, so we are together more than when I worked for someone else.

What is the key to a successful catering business? In addition to a wide range of experience, the key is to give the staff the tools they need to be successful. A crucial skill is to know which people to put together for a winning team. Even though someone has great skills, he or she must be positioned with the right people to make a successful team.

Noteable Event Productions actively participates in three professional associations: the American Culinary Federation (ACF) Chicago Chefs of Cuisine, the Illinois Restaurant Association, and the Society of Foodservice Management.

My advice to you: If you don't like one aspect of the industry, try another, but don't leave the industry. Get as much experience in all aspects of the industry as you can—then pick the one that you like best. Don't be afraid to try a new venue.

Establishing Standard Food Production Procedures

1

Inside This Chapter

- The Importance of Standards for Controlling Production Volume
- Establishing Standards for Controlling Production Volume
- Using Standard Procedures to Control Production Volume
- Sales History and Forecasting
- Knowledge and Skills Needed by Food Production Employees

After completing this chapter, you should be able to:

- Explain the importance of standards for controlling production volume.
- Establish standards for controlling production volume.
- List and describe standard procedures that enable managers to gain control over production volume.
- Describe methods for gathering data from which a sales history is developed.
- List and describe knowledge and skill levels needed by food production employees.

Test Your Knowledge

1. **True or False:** Standard operating procedures (SOPs) should be used as guidelines for training new staff members. *(See p. 10.)*

2. **True or False:** Standardized recipes, product specification sheets, and menu descriptions are some of the control functions a manager can use to ensure correct production. *(See p. 4.)*

3. **True or False:** POS stands for "point of service." *(See p. 12.)*

4. **True or False:** A sales history is necessary to predict future production volume. *(See p. 12.)*

5. **True or False:** An intermediate food production employee has managerial and supervisory duties during production (preparing, cooking, etc.). *(See p. 14.)*

Key Terms

Back of the house

Conversion

Forecasting

Front of the house

Par level

Plating

Point-of-sale (POS) system

Portion size

Prep sheet

Product specification sheet

Production volume

Sales history

Standard operating procedure (SOP)

Standardized recipe

Yield

Introduction

Consistent production of food is critical to the success of any restaurant or foodservice operation. An establishment needs to set standards for producing quality dishes and have a process in place so all employees can implement those standards.

The first step is to set standards for recipes. The recipes are then used to create product specification sheets for vendors. Once standards are set for individual recipes, management creates procedures to ensure that, no matter who is working on a given day or what quantity is produced, the quality of the items remains the same. These procedures are incorporated into tools called prep sheets and menu descriptions.

In this chapter, you will learn how these tools are established and used so that any establishment in which you work can run smoothly and profitably.

Restaurant and foodservice operations also need to respond to various changes such as customers' tastes and the emphasis on healthier eating. All employees need to help gather data for a sales history so the establishment can respond to these changes. The **sales history** is a tool that restaurants use to keep a record of what was sold each day.

Equally important to the success of an operation are the skills of its employees. As part of this chapter, you will learn about the various skill levels of food production employees and how they relate to the daily production routine of an operation.

The Importance of Standards for Controlling Production Volume

One of the goals of any successful restaurant manager is to satisfy the operation's customers while still making a profit. To do this, an operation must have standard procedures for producing its menu items. Food production standards are designed to ensure that customers receive the same quality of food on each visit to the operation, which, in turn, helps ensure the success of the business by building the operation's reputation, creating regular customers, and keeping costs consistent.

In larger operations with multiple locations, these standard procedures ensure that the meal served in one location is comparable to the same meal in another location with regard to quality, taste, and presentation.

Establishing Standards for Controlling Production Volume

Food production standards are typically created at the establishment by its managers and chefs, although a larger operation or chain might set these standards for all the organization's units at its headquarters. Regardless of where they are designed, these procedures must reflect the operation's sales histories, its capacity to produce food, and the skills of its employees. Managers who set food production standards should base their decisions on these factors, as well as their knowledge of customers' preferences.

One of the most important uses of food production standards is to control production volume. Controlling **production volume** is a critical function for an operation. It allows the operation to produce food in sufficient quantities at a specified level of quality, without having excess unused product.

Exhibit 1a

Notice how the prep sheet, spec sheet, and menu description each give a different perspective of a menu item.

Exhibit 1b

Standardized Recipe Format

Item: **Squash Risotto**

Recipe yield: **18.75 quarts**

Number of portions: **50**

Standard portion size: **1½ cups**

Amount	Ingredient	Procedure
1 gal	Chicken stock	1. Bring stock to a boil in a steam-jacketed kettle. Then reduce heat to low. Cover and keep hot. Reserve.
3 oz	Olive oil	
12 oz	Onions	2. Heat oil to 350°F in fry pan. Sauté onion and garlic in oil until translucent, about 4 minutes.
1 clove	Garlic, minced	
2¼ lb	Arborio rice	3. Add rice to onion. Stir and cook 3 minutes.
1½ c	Water	4. Add water and cook until water evaporates. Reduce temperature and add broth slowly, 2 cups at a time (broth reserved from earlier step). Stir very often but not constantly. Do not let the pan become dry before adding more broth.
12 oz	Butter	
12 oz	Cheese, grated	
4 lb	Butternut squash, cooked and puréed	
		5. Cook and stir rice until rice is al dente and mixture is creamy (about 20 minutes).
		6. Toss in squash and serve.

In-House Control Functions

No matter its size, every restaurant or foodservice operation should use the following tools to control production volume:

- Standardized recipes

- Product specification sheets

- Menu descriptions

- Preparation sheets

Each menu item in your operation should go through a process that defines a plan for controlling its production volume. That plan should include all of the tools listed above, tailored individually to each item. (See *Exhibit 1a.*)

Standardized Recipes

Standardized recipes list the ingredients and quantities needed for a menu item, as well as the methods used to produce it and its appropriate portion size. Standardized recipes are written in consistent language that refers to uniform production elements, so employees can exactly reproduce these recipes as needed. A standardized recipe might also include (see *Exhibit 1b*):

- **Ingredient details—** Grades and brands of products needed, precise descriptions, etc.

- **Correct weights and measures of the ingredients**

- **Equipment and tools needed**—Specifies everything from pots to utensils, information that is particularly important to kitchen workers. Consider the difference between a spatula needed to turn one portion of fish (6-inch spatula) and one needed to turn 150 pieces (16-inch offset fish spatula).

- **Volume to be produced**—Depends partly on portion size, or the size of an item's individual serving, such as "four ounces of chicken"

- **Time required to make the item**

- **Storage and preparation information**—Includes information on thawing, what types of cuts need to be made, etc.

- **Cooking methods to be used**—Examples include blanching, sautéing, deep-frying, etc.

The more information you can give to employees, the more likely it is they will repeatedly produce an item correctly. A standardized recipe avoids the creative or personal preference approach to producing menu items. No one in the operation should include his or her personal preferences after standardized recipes have been set by management, nor should anyone be allowed to substitute amounts, ingredients, or cooking techniques.

Additionally, although standardized recipes can be written by hand, a computer-generated system for maintaining recipes has its advantages. By using a computerized version, managers and chefs can easily convert standardized recipes into price lists for purchasing, menu plans, and kitchen operations. Additionally, computerized recipes help reduce the chance for error compared to handwritten versions (where calculations might be incorrect), and they ease the workload of the chef by providing recipe conversions for daily production. (See *Exhibit 1c.*)

Exhibit 1c

Computerized Standardized Recipe

File Edit Ingredient Help

Title: Baked Apples
Description:
Servings: 8   Yield (Amount/Unit):

		Amount	Unit	Ingredient	Preparation
▸1	I	8		apples, red or golden delicious	
▸2	I	6	ounces	raisins	
▸3	I	1½	tablespoons	orange zest	
▸4	I	4	ounces	brown sugar	
▸5					
▸6					
▸7					
▸8					
▸9					

Directions | Notes | Serving Ideas | Time | More Info | Nutrition

▸1	Rinse and core apples. The peels should be scored or removed.	▸
▸2	Plump the raisins by soaking them in boiling water for 10 min., then drain raisins thoroughly.	▸
▸3	Combine the raisins, orange zest, and brown sugar. Fill the cavity of each apple with this mixture.	▸
▸4	Stand the apples in a shallow baking dish. Add water so it measures about 1/2 inch deep.	▸
▸5	Bake the apples at 375º F for 15 min.	▸
▸6	Reduce the temperature to 300º F and continue baking until the apples are tender but still whole (1 hour).	▸
▸7	Occasionally, baste the apples with the liquid from the baking dish.	▸
▸8		▸
▸9		▸

Converting Standard Recipes

One task that is performed frequently with a standardized recipe is conversion. A standard recipe always gives the **yield,** or number of servings produced based on a stated portion size. **Conversion** means to change a recipe from one yield to another.

On any given day, you might expect to sell more or less of an item than its recipe's yield specifies, which means you must convert all the ingredients in the recipe to a new yield. For example, Goldie's Steakhouse expects to sell twenty-four servings of Steak Vesuvio on weekday nights and thirty-six servings on weekend nights, based on past sales history. So each weekend, the managing chef at Goldie's must convert all the ingredients of Steak Vesuvio to a larger number. Once again, computerized standard recipes are easier to convert, particularly when large quantities are needed. Bear in mind, however, that not all recipes can be increased by a third or more without changing the quality. (See Chapter 7 for more information about quality.)

Product Specification Sheets

A **product specification sheet** lists precise descriptions of important characteristics that a particular product should have. These characteristics should meet certain standards of quality, cost, taste, volume, and condition upon delivery. Product specification sheets are written by an operation's management team, which in a larger organization would include the executive chef and the purchasing department.

Product specifications have many purposes:

- Ensure and control quantity, quality standards, and costs

- Educate managers and purchasers about the operation's standards

- Help avoid misunderstandings between the operation and its suppliers

- Allow staff members to place orders without jeopardizing the quality of the operation's products and services

- Serve as the basis for bid writing to new or current suppliers

Product specifications can be short; for example, a recipe may suggest that a particular brand of soy sauce be used. In other situations, the spec sheet might be several pages long to ensure that strict requirements are followed, such as those needed in hospitals or by the military. *Exhibit 1d* provides examples of product specification sheets at an operation.

Exhibit 1d

Examples of Product Specification Sheets

Fish and Seafood

Exact name: Red Snapper

Origin: Florida Gulf Coast

Product condition: Fresh, 1–3 days off boat

Product form: Drawn

Size: 1–3 lb

Packing medium: Ice

Refrigeration: Maximum temperature 30°F to 34°F (-1°C to 1°C)

Other conditions: No "off" odors, clear and full eyes, bright red gills, firm flesh

Meat

Exact name: New York strip steak

Product number: IMPS #1180

Quality grade: USDA Top of the Grade Choice

Yield grade: Cut from USDA Yield Grade 2 carcass

Age: Wet aged 14–21 days

Portion size: 12-oz portion cut

Packaging form: Vacuum packed

Packaging procedure: Layered pack

Package unit: 10–12 lb boxes

Variance allowed in size: Weight variance from 12 oz : ± 1 oz

Refrigeration: Chilled, maximum temperature 36°F (2°C)

Menu Descriptions

Menu descriptions show all the ingredients, portion size, and size count in a dish on one piece of paper or poster. Just as a standardized recipe is used to consistently create individual recipes, a menu description is a standardization of an entire menu item, or plated item, that is served to a customer. **Plating** is how an item is served, including the dish, garnish, sauce, and arrangement of food items on a plate.

Menu descriptions are useful tools for all employees in a restaurant. As shown in *Exhibit 1e* on the next page, each menu item's description includes a photograph, its ingredients, special equipment and tools needed, cooking method used, and the way in which the item is served. Note, however, that menu descriptions never show the procedures to make a particular dish.

A menu description helps the kitchen staff consistently prepare meals in numerous ways:

- Illustrates a menu item so it matches a standardized recipe

- Shows the volume of items on a plate

- Displays special presentation considerations

- Allows staff to see the distinction between different-sized portions

- Helps set up a standard operating procedure (SOP) based on a menu item

- Can include a point-of-sale (POS) item number, if used, resulting in fewer mistakes

The front-of-the-house staff, especially servers, can also benefit from menu descriptions in these ways:

- To explain ingredients, especially if customers are allergic to specific ingredients

■ To explain specials—for example, a restaurant may regularly offer mushroom soup, which consists of button and shiitake mushrooms, but if the restaurant then creates a "special" mushroom soup, the menu description would explain that it is made of different kinds of mushrooms

Menu descriptions are also valuable to management:

■ A POS number generates information about the ingredients in a menu item that can be used to analyze sales data.

■ Menu descriptions can be used to train new kitchen and server staff.

■ Revision dates are important when evaluating an entire menu.

Exhibit 1e

Menu Descriptions

	Menu Item	Ingredients	Equipment and Tools	Cooking Method	Serving Method
	Bowtie Pasta with Basil and Plum Tomatoes POS 404	Pasta, plum tomatoes, garlic, fresh basil	9-inch saute pan, 10-inch tongs, stovetop	Sautéed with olive oil, simmered in chicken stock, tossed with pasta, topped with Parmesan cheese	Deep soup bowl
	Bruschetta POS 245	Bread, olive oil, tomato-basil salsa	Baking sheet, 9-inch tongs, brush, convection oven heated to 350°F (177°C)	Bread is grilled and brushed with olive oil, served with tomato-basil salsa	Appetizer plate
	Caesar Salad POS 110	Romaine lettuce, Caesar dressing, homemade croutons	Caesar salad mixing bowl, 9-inch tongs	Toss salad with dressing, garnish with croutons	Salad bowl with salad tongs
	Curry Chicken Puff POS 560	Puff pastry, chicken filling, curry, butter, flour, Dijon mustard, red onions	For curry chicken filling—9-inch sauté pan, 9-inch tongs, stovetop; for puff pastry—marble work surface, rolling pin	Fill puff pastry with curry chicken filling, bake until golden brown	Entrée plate

Preparation Sheets

A **prep sheet,** short for preparation sheet, sets the standards for basic items to have on hand in an establishment. The prep sheet, shown in *Exhibit 1f*, ensures that enough meats, sauces, garnishes, and other basic food items are available at all times.

Exhibit 1f

Sample Lunch Prep Sheet with Par Levels

Prep Sheet for ___Grill station___

Item	On Hand	Par Level Mon–Thu	Par Level Fri–Sat	Initials
8-oz steaks		50	80	
12-oz steaks		40	100	
New York strip steak		25	35	
Burger patties		90	150	
Vegetables		1 half-size hotel pan	2 half-size hotel pans	
Shrimp skewers		60	120	
Green pepper sauce		3 pints	3 quarts	
Au jus		1 quart	3 quarts	
Habanero mayonnaise		1 pint	2 pints	
BLT setups		90	150	
Cheese (Swiss, mozzarella, colby, jack)		30 slices each	90 slices each	
Duck glace		1 pint	3 pints	

The **par level** is an important part of the prep sheet. This is the quantity of items needed for a particular food item, for each day's anticipated number of servings. The par level can fluctuate, depending on the day of the week, or if special events are scheduled. Note that in *Exhibit 1f* different amounts are projected for weekdays and weekends.

Par levels are based on the yield of a recipe. Most establishments allow a buffer between the yield specified in the standardized recipe and the amount ordered and par levels. The buffer accounts for food portions that may become unusable. It also accounts for different quantities that may be used during various shifts or day parts, ensuring there are always enough ingredients on hand.

The prep sheet is used daily at the beginning of each shift. Typically, beginner and intermediate kitchen staff remove food from the cooler or shelves, and enter information on the prep sheet about each product on hand. The kitchen management staff will then verify and sign off on the par level amounts.

Using Standard Procedures to Control Production Volume

In the previous section, you learned how to develop standards that can help control production volume. Utilizing these standards, your organization can create **standard operating procedures (SOPs)** that will guide the activities your employees perform while doing their jobs as well as be used for training new employees. As the manager, you must ensure that your employees are performing these procedures correctly.

Below is the procedure a food production staff typically would use in daily food production. Note that once a recipe has been selected and the details have been standardized, the tools are used in a slightly different order.

1. Each day, start planning for the next day by using sales histories to forecast the number of anticipated servings. The manager converts the recipe to the appropriate quantities and usually calculates different amounts for busier or slower times. The manager uses the portions needed to derive the numbers on the prep sheets and par levels that should be on hand.

2. As the experienced kitchen workers arrive at work, they begin their daily tasks as instructed by the sous chef and management. The following tools help them prepare and serve food:

   ☐ **Product specification sheets**—To maintain consistency and product quality, ensure that the ingredient specifications are being followed. Conduct spot checks to compare the products being used against those listed in the spec sheet. It is not acceptable for your employees to substitute a product if they run out of the product specified on the sheet.

   ☐ **Preparation sheets**—Review the prep sheets daily to ensure that the par levels for basic items are on hand and meet the specified standard. If par levels are consistently not being met, then check the purchase orders and reevaluate the current purchasing procedures. Par levels must be maintained in order to control production volume.

   ☐ **Standardized recipes**—Ensure that every dish prepared in the kitchen has been produced using a standardized recipe. Periodically check on employees to see if they are using the correct ingredients and preparing the dish as spelled out in the recipe. You may also decide to verify that the final product meets the required standards based on the recipe.

☐ **Menu descriptions**—Periodically check plates before they leave the kitchen. Specifically, ensure that each plate resembles the picture in the menu description. If the portions are not exact, check to see if the right utensils are being used. Make sure that your menu descriptions are accessible and visible to everyone who needs them. You may also decide to periodically quiz the servers and kitchen staff about the exact portions of a finished menu item.

Using the Tools to Plan New Menu Items

The basic tools for restaurant and foodservice establishments—standardized recipes, specification sheets, preparation sheets, and menu descriptions—are used differently when planning new menu items than they are when running daily operations.

Planning a new menu item is initiated as needed, which may be based on sales history, customer requests, and other conditions. When an operation plans a new menu item, management creates the standardized recipe first. Then they create the specification sheet and preparation sheet for purchasing and daily operations. The menu description is prepared when the dish and its accompaniments are completed.

Exhibit 1g

Front-of-the-house preshift meeting

Daily Operations

There is a rhythm to a restaurant or foodservice establishment that begins long before customers arrive. To make sure all the correct operating procedures are put into place, regular meetings should be scheduled by management with servers, chefs, and food production employees. You should determine how to schedule meetings for both the front of the house and the back of the house. **Front of the house** refers to the staff members who work in the front of a restaurant, such as the servers, *maître d'*, and host or hostess. (See *Exhibit 1g*.) **Back of the house** refers to kitchen employees and management staff.

A meeting before each shift is absolutely necessary for the success of an operation. Including all employees in these meetings allows them to ask questions and builds loyalty to the establishment— a key to retaining good employees.

At the daily meeting, the staff can discuss the specials for the day. You can also talk about expected customer volume and any planned special events, such as a holiday promotion or private party.

Additionally, you can introduce changes in standardized recipes, or procedures needed for an increase in expected customers. As much business information as possible should be integrated into these regular meetings. When employees have an understanding of past and projected sales, they will be more likely to work to meet these numbers. Employees will also understand the reasons for additional work and will be more likely to try to meet these expectations.

Activity

Change in Plans

You are the manager of the Beyond the Blue restaurant. You are preparing for the preshift meeting for your staff. You notice that there is a luncheon for thirty-five people today, in addition to the normal lunch customers. Beyond the Blue will be serving its well-known Starlight Chicken with Rice, served with three ounces of light tomato sauce.

1 What changes must you alert your staff to during the meeting?

_____

_____

2 What must be changed on the prep sheet, and what else must be prepared?

_____

_____

Sales History and Forecasting

Profitable food production depends on correct forecasting. **Forecasting** predicts the number of guests an operation will serve in a given time period, which in turn guides the kitchen staff's preparation sheets for that same period. Good forecasting is based on accurate sales histories. The sales history tracks the number of guests and their food choices for a specific period of time. The sales history also helps to identify trends that may be seasonal or caused by holidays or special events.

It is critical that your establishment has processes in place to accurately gather sales histories. There are two recognized methods for gathering this information: point-of-sale systems and server input of customer orders. When used properly, these methods will produce accurate histories, but keep in mind that forecasts are not always exact. For example, bad weather and other events beyond an establishment's control can affect revenue.

Point-of-Sale (POS) Systems

Many restaurants have computer systems—called **point-of-sale (POS) systems**—that servers use to enter customers' orders. (See *Exhibit 1h.*) The advantage of a POS system is that once

Exhibit 1h

At many establishments, servers input customers' orders into a POS system.

the order is placed into the system, it generates multiple types of sales information. It can track the ingredients in each dish and break down costs accordingly. A POS system also tracks orders by the hour, so that staffing and equipment usage can be assigned accordingly. For example, a usage summary breaks down ingredients for each item in the inventory. (See *Exhibit 1i*.)

Server Input of Customer Orders

Today, POS systems calculate sales information as servers enter orders. Traditionally, however, restaurants manually collected all guest checks and charted information about total covers, or individual diners, total sales, itemized sales, and time of purchase.

Server input is still a primary source of sales information. Servers enter orders, including special requests, for each customer served. At the end of the day, after the cash register is closed, the manager and chef can review the day's sales and compare it to those of the previous week and month.

Exhibit 1i

Usage Summary

USAGE SUMMARY

JB's Eatery
1423 St. John's Ave.
Harper, CT 06039
USA

Store ID: JBSEATERY

From: Monday, April 03, 2007
To: Sunday, May 27, 2007

Gross Sales: $520,278.67
Customer Count: 0.00

Actual Cost of Sales: $193,028.60 — 37.10%
Ideal Cost of Sales: $172,402.00 — 33.14%
Difference: $20,626.60 — 3.96%
Total Ending Inventory Value: $22,586.24

Item Description	Opening Inventory	Period Purchase	Ending Inventory	Actual Usage	Ideal Usage	Difference	Difference Cost	Ending Inv. Value
Add-On								
Soup Beef Base Paste	2.500 1 lb.	0.000 1 lb.	1.000 1 lb.	1.500 1 lb.	6.5954 1 lb.	−5.0951 lb.	($35.57)	$6.98
Add-On Group Totals		Actual: $10.47 — 0.00%			Ideal: $46.04 — 0.01%		($35.57)	$6.98
Appetizer								
Clam Nectar	16.400 1.31lt.	24.00 1.31lt.	13.200 1.31lt.	27.200 1.31lt.	15.9000 1.31lt.	11.300 1.31lt.	$24.19	$27.86
Clams Whole Baby	11.400 can	24.00 can	13.200 can	22.200 can	15.900 can	6.300 can	$24.77	$51.92
Pita Chips	0.000 lb.	210.00 lb.	25.875 lb.	184.125 lb.	84.750 0 lb.	99.375 lb.	$149.79	$39.00
Quiche Mini	0.000 200p	1.00 200p	0.000 200p	1.000 200p	0.000 200p	1.000 200p	$66.36	$0.00
Appetizer Group Totals		Actual: $489.40 — 0.09%			Ideal: $224.29 — 0.04%		$265.11	$118.78
Beverage								
Coffee Decaf P/C	74.000 2.25pk	160.00 2.25pk	70.000 2.25pk	164.000 2.25pk	0.000 2.25k	164.000 2.25pk	$80.02	$42.36
Coffee Whole Bean	30.000 bag2#	108.00 bag2#	21.000 bag2#	117.000 bag2#	109.275 0 bag2#	7.725 bag2#	$83.64	$227.48
Beverage Group Totals		Actual: $1,346.75 — 0.26%			Ideal: $1,183.09 — 0.23%		$163.66	$269.86
Bread								
Bread	546.000 loaf	7560.00 loaf	252.000 loaf	7854.000 loaf	3220.5000 loaf	4633.500 loaf	$2,315.30	$123.90
Bread French Loaf	73.000 loaf	679.00 loaf	47.000 loaf	705.000 loaf	921.6475 loaf	−216.648 loaf	($363.87)	$77.48
Bread Marble Rye Loaf	14.500 loaf	44.00 loaf	8.500 loaf	50.000 loaf	41.2500 loaf	8.750 loaf	$41.59	$39.00
Bread Sunflower Loaf	20.000 loaf	216.00 loaf	18.500 loaf	217.500 loaf	188.9375 loaf	28.563 loaf	$111.11	$71.04
Bread Hamburger Sourdough	180.000 bun	2400.00 bun	120.000 bun	2460.000 bun	2355.0000 bun	105.000 bun	$37.50	$42.18
Muffin English	8.500 pak.	24.00 pak.	15.000 pak.	17.500 pak.	12.6667 pak.	4.833 pak.	$70.87	$281.70
Roll French Par Baked	164.000 roll	1490.00 roll	0.000 roll	1654.000 roll	1071.0000 roll	583.000 roll	$81.84	$0.00
Bread Group Totals		Actual: $17,559.71 — 1.45%			Ideal: $5,265.37 — 1.01%		$2,294.34	$635.34
Canned Goods								
Artichoke Hearts Qrted	3.160 2.42L	12.00 2.42L	2.545 2.42L	12.615 2.42L	7.6635 2.42L	4.952 2.42L	$43.20	$21.63
Beans Black Whole	27.000 540ml	120.00 540ml	37.000 540ml	110.000 540ml	69.0526 540ml	40.947 540ml	$36.03	$33.19
Escargot	4.540 cn 28oz	24.00 cn 28oz	1.323 cn 28oz	27.217 cn 28oz	27.7500 cn 28oz	−0.533 cn 28oz	($2.45)	$6.07
Marmalade Orange	4.429 750ml	0.00 750ml	2.000 750ml	2.429 750ml	2.1786 750ml	0.250 750ml	$0.87	$6.98

Print Date: 07/14/07

Page 1 of 12

Knowledge and Skills Needed by Food Production Employees

You have seen throughout this chapter how strong standardized food production procedures will help an operation control its production volume and ensure the making of quality, consistent menu items for its customers to enjoy. Even with these procedures, however, your operation cannot get very far without a skilled team of foodservice workers. To be successful, an operation must have a production team with a variety of specialized skills at all levels.

Exhibit 1j lists the skills needed at five stages in the flow of food. For each stage, there are examples of tasks. Note how the skills become more complex as you progress from beginner to intermediate to advanced for each stage. Also note that more initiative is required to learn new techniques from one level to the next.

Exhibit 1j

Knowledge and Skills Required for Experience Levels

Stage	Beginner	Intermediate	Advanced
Preparing	Cleaning and cutting vegetables, parboiling pasta for line	Prepping line items, which are more expensive and used daily; for example, cutting and marinating portion-sized steaks, preportioning fish	Working on special menu items, creating standardized recipes, preparing creative sauce solutions, adding last-minute touches for garnishes
Cooking	Following standardized basic recipes for simple production; for example, stocks, starches, vegetables of the day, puff pastries; assemble ingredients; prepare garnishes with direction	Following standardized recipes for more complex dishes; for example, Hollandaise sauce; executing menu items on the line for specific service times; for example, lunch cook, fry cook	Creating and following standardized recipes, training staff on using standardized recipes and standardized operating procedures, supervising beginner and intermediate cooks to ensure proper procedures while executing standardized recipes
Holding, Cooling, Reheating	Following proper sanitary standard procedures, is supervised and signed out for proper completion by manager	Following proper sanitary standard procedures, is supervised and signed out for proper completion by manager, acts as role model for beginners	Developing HACCP program or sanitation and cleaning SOPs, signing all staff out after proper cleaning and closing of stations

Activity

Tasks by Skill Level

Determine the skill level for the following tasks as beginner (B), intermediate (I), or advanced (A).

1 Preparing salad _____   **4** Preparing a side dish _____

2 Making stock _____   **5** Baking bread _____

3 Cutting portions _____   **6** Maintaining par levels _____

Summary

Setting and maintaining standard food production procedures are critical to producing food products of consistently high quality. The process starts by preparing standardized recipes. Standardized recipes have a consistent format so that anyone who uses them will produce the same result each time. Standardized recipes also allow for scaling to different production quantities.

Standardized recipes are the basis for product specification sheets. These sheets list as many details as possible for a particular food product.

Chefs create prep sheets that list par levels of food items and sauces. The food production employees must maintain these ideal levels on a daily basis.

Menu descriptions help explain ingredients and presentation so servers and other staff can understand each dish. They are also used in training new employees.

Sales histories, based on server input of customer orders, are critical to forecasting anticipated customers and dishes. POS systems can track multiple items from this input.

The skills and knowledge levels of food production employees are grouped into beginner, intermediate, and advanced levels. Employees should always note what is needed to move to the next level.

Activity

New Menu Item

Laura, the executive chef of Steak Heaven, a midsize restaurant, reads the sales history daily. She consistently compares sales of specials to regular items. She notices that after four months, people are ordering less of the Filet Mignon Steak, which has been popular for years. She also sees that when the restaurant offers the Skirt Steak special, which is much more profitable, it sells out quickly.

She confers with the sous chef about equipment needs, product changes, and preparation time of each dish during peak times. She talks with servers who know the regular customers well. After a meeting with the staff, she decides to add the Skirt Steak to the regular menu.

1 What changes in production need to occur now that the Skirt Steak special is a regular item?

_____

_____

_____

_____

_____

_____

_____

_____

2 What needs to be done so that all staff members know about the addition and how it may affect operations?

_____

_____

_____

_____

_____

_____

_____

_____

3 How and when should this change be made?

_____

_____

_____

_____

_____

_____

_____

Review Your Learning

1 Which is *not* a component of a standardized recipe?

A. Name of the recipe

B. Par level

C. Portion size

D. Yield of the completed recipe

2 Which is least likely to occur in a restaurant as it implements standardized recipes?

A. All cooks are trained to prepare the new recipe.

B. Standardization of production is implemented as part of the operational procedure.

C. When new recipes are created, they are immediately written down in a standardized recipe format.

D. An intermediate cook is allowed to create a new, popular dish.

3 All of these result from failing to use a standardized recipe *except*

A. incorrect production volume.

B. incomplete product.

C. inconsistent product.

D. ingredient running out.

4 Which item is *not* necessary on a product specification sheet?

A. Menu item in which the product will be used

B. Name of the product

C. Vendor's packaging size

D. Quality standards

5 Which tool is used by front-of-the-house staff, back-of-the-house staff, and management?

A. Menu description

B. Prep sheet

C. Product specification sheet

D. Standardized recipe

6 The number of servings produced by a standardized recipe is the

A. par level.

B. portion size.

C. production volume.

D. yield.

7 Which is *not* a sufficient product specification?

A. Yellow beefsteak tomatoes, 1cs/4×5, top quality

B. Ketchup, 1cs/12/24-ounce bottles

C. Mayonnaise

D. USDA prime, American, rack of lamb, 1cs/12/2 each

Notes

Product Quality— Know Your Product

2

After completing this chapter, you should be able to:

- Explain how food products are inspected and graded.
- Explain the characteristics of quality in each major food category: produce, seafood, meat, poultry, dairy products, and dry goods.
- Describe new methods of packaging food.

Test Your Knowledge

1 **True or False:** Fruit and vegetables are graded before they are shipped to packinghouses. *(See p. 22.)*

2 **True or False:** A meat quality grade measures the proportion of useable meat. *(See p. 28.)*

3 **True or False:** Dry goods, such as flour and sugar, are *not* graded. *(See p. 34.)*

4 **True or False:** Operations that market their seafood items as "fresh caught" can use frozen seafood in preparing menu items. *(See pp. 24–25.)*

5 **True or False:** Since poultry age affects the tenderness of the bird, older birds should *not* be used by restaurant and foodservice operations. *(See p. 31.)*

6 **True or False:** *Sous vide* food is vacuum-packed in individual pouches that can be heated for service in the establishment. *(See p. 44.)*

Key Terms

Brown sugar	Granulated sugar	Reduced
Confectioners' sugar	Homogenization	Shortening
Conformation	Hydrogenated	Tempered
Dairy products	Leavening	Tenderloin
Dark meat	Margarine	Value-added
Dry yeast	Meal	White meat
Fermentation	Pasteurization	Wholesomeness
Fermented	Perishable	Yeast
Fresh yeast	Poultry class	Yield grade
Gluten	Quality grade	

Introduction

Standards, quality, control, maintenance—these are all words that you will become very accustomed to hearing when managing a restaurant or foodservice operation. In Chapter 1, you learned about the standards that are set for quality food offerings. In this chapter, you will learn how and why food selection is conducted so that you can establish those standards.

Food selection begins with assessing the quality that each product must have in order to meet recipe requirements. The product's intended use, market form, processing method, storage needs, and many other variables are factors that will aid your decision. In many cases, the quality of the product is assessed by the federal government through inspection or grading. While quality grades are voluntary, grading the product also provides an official stamp of approval backed by firm quality standards. Understanding what to look for in quality food ingredients, and knowing the quality grades and what they mean will help you to use ingredients efficiently in your recipes.

Once you are familiar with the characteristics of food products, you will be better prepared to handle them during preparation and cooking. Understanding the variety of products, their formats, and their qualities will encourage you to explore different ingredients and incorporate them into your recipes.

Know Your Food Products: Food Inspections and Grading

To produce quality menu items, you need to know the features of each dish, how to bring out characteristic traits of certain ingredients during preparation and cooking, and how to preserve these ingredients' qualities. Understanding the qualities of basic ingredients will also help you select the items that best suit your recipes.

Additional advantages of taking the time to learn the qualities of the ingredients used in your operation include:

- Being able to determine if you can accommodate customer requests when asked to customize an order

- Being able to choose the correct ingredients to ensure your operation uses products efficiently, thus saving money in the long run

Most of the food discussed in this chapter is **perishable,** which means it spoils or deteriorates rapidly. The majority of the food you will serve to your customers, and thus the largest part of your revenue, is perishable. Examples of perishable food, which will be discussed in detail in later sections, include:

- Produce
- Seafood
- Meat
- Poultry and eggs
- Dairy products—milk, butter, and cheese

Nonperishable food items, including various baking ingredients and herbs and spices, are important to the quality of menu items and will also be discussed. Although these items are not typically formally inspected, there are levels of quality that you must understand to ensure you make the right choices for your operation's dishes.

Produce

Since the 1990s, many consumers have shown renewed interest in eating fresh fruit and vegetables. Many celebrity chefs have also introduced the concept of raw food—uncooked food—into their recipes. Serving fruit or vegetables in heavy sauces, frying vegetables in oil, and adding sugar to fruit are all methods that alter or reduce the amount of vitamins, minerals, and nutrients available; these methods also affect the quality of fruit and vegetables.

Grades of Produce

In the United States, fruit and vegetables that are grown in orchards and fields are graded, while produce grown in greenhouses are given slightly different grades. The United States Department of Agriculture (USDA) assigns grades to over eighty-five kinds of fresh fruit and vegetables, from artichokes to watermelon. Items are typically graded before they are shipped to packinghouses and then to vendors.

Depending on the fruit or vegetable, the USDA has a scale of two to four grades, which generally ranges from U.S. Extra Fancy to U.S. No. 2. Grades are assigned according to a number of guidelines. For example, fresh tomatoes are graded according to size, color, and any defects, and may be assigned one of four grades: USDA No. 1, USDA No. 2, USDA No. 3, or combination.

You can review the various grading specifications for fresh fruit and vegetables at *www.ams.usda.gov/standards/stanfrfv.htm.* Note that there are separate standards for fruit and vegetables intended for processing.

Choosing the Right Grade of Produce

You probably will not be able to memorize all the grade standards for produce, but a vendor can easily show you the differences between the grades for any fruit or vegetable supplied. You can order samples of any fruit or vegetable, do your own cutting, and develop your own grade sheets for a certain fruit or vegetable. Keep notes for your menu items stating which grades are acceptable. Write this information on your bid sheet, and calculate the difference a particular grade will have on the price of a menu item. Depending on the menu item, you might be surprised to find that you can use a lower-grade product yet still provide the necessary quality for your standardized recipe.

Activity

Apples

Locate the grading standards for apples at *www.ams.usda.gov/standards/apples.pdf.* **Answer the questions below, based on the grades.**

1 Is U.S. Extra Fancy the best and most profitable choice for an apple pie?

_____

_____

_____

2 Is U.S. Utility the best choice to serve whole at a breakfast buffet or in a fruit basket?

_____

_____

_____

3 Write a use for each of the grades.

_____

_____

_____

Seafood

Seafood is divided into two major categories: fish and shellfish. Fish have a backbone and can live in fresh water or in the ocean. Shellfish have an outer shell but no backbone and are found primarily in salt water. Both types of seafood are available in fresh or processed forms.

■ **Fish** can be classified according to their shape, either round or flat. **Round fish** have a round body shape and one eye on each side of the head, and they swim upright in salt water or fresh water. Some examples are cod, sea bass, mahi-mahi, tuna, and skate. **Flatfish** are oval or flat in shape and have two eyes on only one side of the head. Examples include flounder, halibut, and turbot.

■ **Shellfish** can be categorized further into crustaceans, mollusks, and cephalopods. *Exhibit 2a* on the next page shows examples of different types of shellfish.

Exhibit 2a

Shellfish

Shellfish Type	Features	Examples
Crustacean	Outer skeleton, jointed appendages	Shrimp, lobster, crab
Mollusk	One or two hard shells	*Univalve* (one shell): abalone *Bivalve* (two hinged shells): clam, oyster, mussel, scallop
Cephalopod	Single internal shell, tentacles	Octopus, squid

Choosing the Right Product

One of the most important decisions you will make about the seafood used in your recipes is which form to purchase. If your operation is a seafood restaurant, then you obviously need to become well versed in the qualities of the fresh seafood featured on your menu. If your operation does not market itself as serving fresh seafood, then you could purchase processed items.

An operation that serves fresh seafood needs to consider these factors:

■ **Intended use**—Before purchasing any type of seafood, you should understand how the kitchen plans to prepare it. Cooking methods should complement a seafood item's characteristics. For example, lean fish do not typically bake well, while fatty fish are not the best choice for deep-frying. You should also consider appearance. Seafood that is broiled or grilled should have an attractive appearance. This is less important for items that will be battered and fried.

■ **Market form**—Vendors can supply seafood to an operation in a number of ways, as shown in *Exhibit 2b*. You should purchase fresh seafood in the market form that best suits your operation's needs. For example, you might buy some types of fish already portioned, saving preparation time and ensuring uniform dishes. On the other hand, you might have kitchen staff with the skills to cut up whole fish. If that is the case, you should consider whether your operation could use the trimmings and bones.

■ **Storage capabilities**—Fresh seafood is highly perishable; therefore, you must have adequate storage facilities for seafood items to ensure as long a shelf life as possible. Temperature control is particularly important, since fresh fish should be received packed in ice and maintained that way in storage.

Careless storage of seafood leads to poor appearance, texture, and odor, as well as food safety issues, all of which ultimately result in wasted product.

■ **Vendor selection**—Considering the vast variety of seafood available, a reliable, reputable supplier is crucial. You should verify that your supplier is an approved food source that has been inspected and is in compliance with all applicable laws. Doing this will help ensure that the seafood you receive is safe and of consistent good quality.

Exhibit 2b

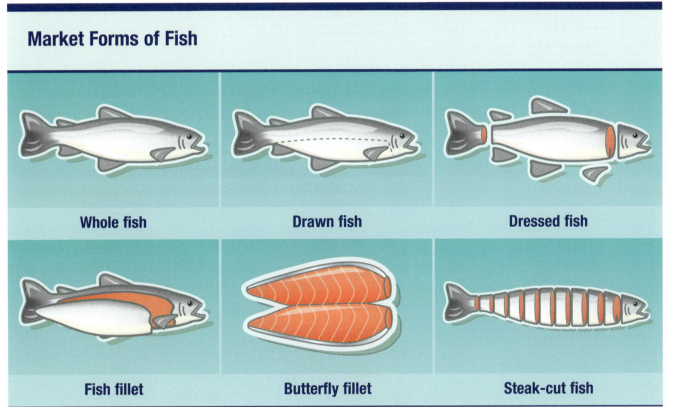

Market Forms of Fish

Whole fish	Drawn fish	Dressed fish
Fish fillet	Butterfly fillet	Steak-cut fish

Processed seafood might be an appropriate choice for your operation if you do not market your menu items as "fresh caught." Customer perception is often negative toward processed food items, but there are many types of processed seafood—from frozen to cured—that offer excellent flavor. Some factors to consider about processed seafood include:

■ **Processing method**—Various types of seafood are available in frozen, canned, and cured forms. The method you choose will depend on the item and how you plan to use it. For example, sardines are often purchased in canned form, while lobster is not. Likewise, an operation might use canned tuna in its sandwiches but purchase frozen tuna steaks for its entrées.

■ **Convenience**—By purchasing processed seafood, an operation might achieve significant cost reductions for equipment and space, as well as reductions in preparation time and labor skills. Yet you must also balance these savings with the increase in unit cost that processed items typically have, as well as the chance that you might decrease the quality of a menu item.

■ **Storage capabilities**—Although processed seafood has a slightly longer shelf life than fresh seafood, it is still highly perishable. Operations must have the appropriate amount of storage equipment and space. Frozen seafood, for example, must be stored frozen. Accidental thawing will result in food safety issues and poor quality.

Seafood Inspections and Grades

The U.S Food and Drug Administration (FDA) monitors interstate fish shipments and also requires fish processors to adopt a Hazard Analysis and Critical Control Point (HACCP) program. Seafood is not inspected when it is caught; instead, inspections are voluntary. Many processors participate in the voluntary seafood inspection program conducted by the U.S. Department of Commerce (USDC). Products that have been inspected under this program carry a Processed Under Federal Inspection (PUFI) mark (see *Exhibit 2c*), indicating that the product is safe and wholesome and has been packed in an establishment that meets the sanitary guidelines required by the National Marine Fisheries Service (NMFS), a division of the USDC.

The NMFS also publishes grades for seafood that has been inspected, though not all types of seafood are included. The grading factors include:

■ Appearance   ■ Flavor

■ Blemishes and damage   ■ Odor

■ Color   ■ Texture

■ Dehydration   ■ Uniformity

Both fresh and processed seafood items can be graded. Items are typically graded as A, B, C, or Below Standard, based on the above factors. Grade A is the highest-quality seafood available. These items have an excellent appearance, good flavor and odor, and are free of blemishes or defects. Grade B items have good quality, but usually have blemishes or other defects. Grade C items have relatively good quality, but these items are only appropriate for dishes that do not require an attractive appearance. Below Standard items do not have good quality.

Exhibit 2c

Seafood Inspection Stamps

PUFI stamp

Fish grade shield

Only Grade A seafood is marked with a stamp. (See *Exhibit 2c.*) Most seafood items sold to restaurant and foodservice establishments are Grade A, but some Grade B products might be appropriate, depending on their usage. To ensure you are ordering the proper quality of seafood items, you should specify which grade you want as part of your buying specifications to the vendor.

Receiving Requirements

Regardless of the type, grade, or form of seafood your operation uses in its recipes, there are some basic receiving principles that will help determine if the items sent from the vendor are of the required quality.

Fresh fish should be packed in self-draining, crushed, or flaked ice. Upon delivery, it should be received at a temperature of 41°F (5°C) or lower. Fresh fish in good condition should also meet these standards:

- Clear eyes
- Firm flesh
- Pleasant, mild scent of ocean or seaweed
- Bright red, moist gills
- Bright skin

Frozen fish that has been thawed or refrozen should be returned. Frozen items must be kept frozen because any unintentional thawing will significantly damage their quality and safety.

Shellfish, in general, can be received live or frozen, with the shells still intact or shucked, and at an internal temperature of 45°F (7°C). Crustaceans, in particular, must be alive upon receipt and at a temperature of 41°F (5°C) or lower. Dead crustaceans must be rejected.

Meat

Meat is often the major part of a restaurant's menu offerings and the central component of a customer's meal choice. The various types of meat available for menu items include beef, veal, pork, and lamb, as well as some processed meats, such as sausages and cold cuts.

Choosing the Right Cut of Meat

Much like seafood menu items, the success of a meat dish often depends on choosing the right form or cut. If you work in an operation that specializes in serving one type of meat, you will need to learn as much as you can about that type. Generally speaking, however, there are some factors you should consider regardless of what kind of meat your operation serves:

Exhibit 2d

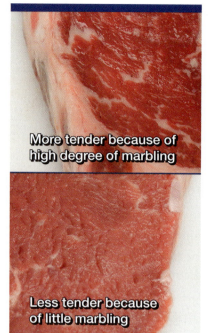

More tender because of high degree of marbling

Less tender because of little marbling

- **Intended use**—As with seafood, some types of meat are better suited to certain cooking methods than others. To ensure a quality menu item, you must match a particular cut with an appropriate cooking method. For example, tough cuts of meat are best cooked by moist heat; broiling would ruin them. For beef products the degree of marbling—flecks of fat within the lean—influences how tender a cut is. In general, a cut of beef with a high degree of marbling is more tender than a cut with little marbling. (See *Exhibit 2d.*)

- **Fabrication needs**—Most restaurant and foodservice operations do not have the space, equipment, or in-house labor skills to butcher whole cuts of meat. Yet some operations purchase certain types of meat in partially fabricated forms, in part to control the cost of buying premium-priced, uniform pieces.

- **Freshness requirements**—Buying meat frozen or in convenience form are both options for various types of meat, since a high-quality frozen product, in many cases, will not appear that different from a fresh product. Storage capabilities are important when choosing these types of items. Any quality lost can usually be attributed to improper handling. For example, items with freezer burn, which forms on loosely wrapped meat that dries out in the freezer, should be avoided because freezer burn reduces the texture and flavor of meat.

Exhibit 2e

Inspection Stamp for Raw Meat

38
U.S.
INSP'D & P'S'D

Meat Inspections

Meat inspection is mandatory in the United States. Inspections, which are done by the USDA, are designed to ensure that the meat is wholesome and the facilities and equipment used to process the meat comply with sanitation standards. Products that have passed the inspection receive the USDA stamp shown in *Exhibit 2e.* These meat products have been approved for **wholesomeness,** which indicates their safety and suitability for human consumption.

Grading

Only meat products that are approved for wholesomeness in inspection may be graded. Apart from wholesomeness, consumers are interested in the meat's quality and may prefer graded products. The quality of meat is based primarily upon its overall flavor characteristics and tenderness.

While voluntary, many processors and packers pay a fee to have meat products graded to ensure their quality. For most types of meat, there are two grades: the quality grade and the yield grade. Some types of meat may carry either a quality grade or a yield grade, while some types of meat may have both. **Quality grade** measures the flavor characteristics of meat products, while **yield grade** measures the proportion of edible or usable meat after being trimmed of bones or fat.

Quality grades include Prime, Choice, Select, Standard, Commercial, Utility, Cutter, Cull, and Canner. *Exhibit 2f* shows each grade and how it describes the quality attributes of the meat product.

Exhibit 2f

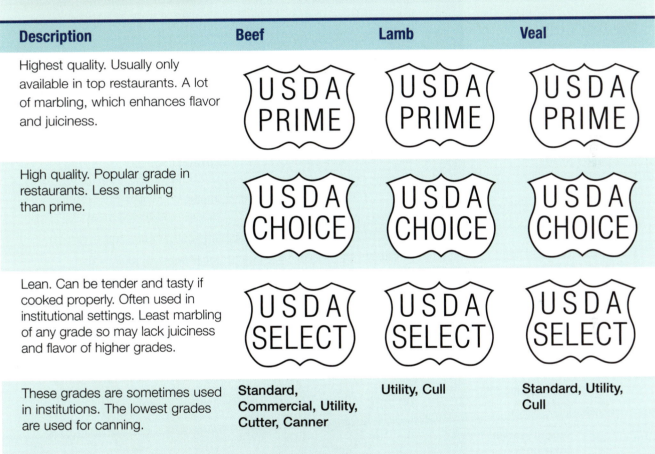

Quality Grades of Meat

Description	Beef	Lamb	Veal
Highest quality. Usually only available in top restaurants. A lot of marbling, which enhances flavor and juiciness.	USDA PRIME	USDA PRIME	USDA PRIME
High quality. Popular grade in restaurants. Less marbling than prime.	USDA CHOICE	USDA CHOICE	USDA CHOICE
Lean. Can be tender and tasty if cooked properly. Often used in institutional settings. Least marbling of any grade so may lack juiciness and flavor of higher grades.	USDA SELECT	USDA SELECT	USDA SELECT
These grades are sometimes used in institutions. The lowest grades are used for canning.	Standard, Commercial, Utility, Cutter, Canner	Utility, Cull	Standard, Utility, Cull

Exhibit 2g

Yield Shield for Pork

At your discretion, you can acquire yield grades for beef, pork, and lamb products. This may be beneficial since the differences in the amount of fat on the outside of the meat can cause the yield of usable product to vary greatly. Unlike other types of meat, pork does not receive a quality grade. Though it is inspected for wholesomeness, pork is a consistent product that is only graded for yield and receives a yield grade stamp, as shown in *Exhibit 2g*.

Poultry

Poultry products include chicken, turkey, and duck. Each product in this category has varying degrees of quality based primarily on the cut, type of meat, nutritional value, or grade and class. Like meat, poultry must also undergo mandated inspection to ensure wholesomeness. In addition to the product's labeling and nutritional value, the processing plant is also inspected for cleanliness and proper handling procedures.

Exhibit 2h

Poultry Cuts

Poultry half
Full-length split down breast and back, producing approximately equal left and right sides

Breast quarter
Half a breast, a wing, and a portion of the back

Leg quarter
A thigh, a drumstick, and a portion of the back

Breast

Tender
any strip of breast meat

Tenderloin
inner pectoral muscle that lies alongside breastbone

Wing

Third section
wing tip

Second section
flat wing tip

First section
wing drumette

Leg

Drumstick

Thigh
also used to make turkey ham

Tail

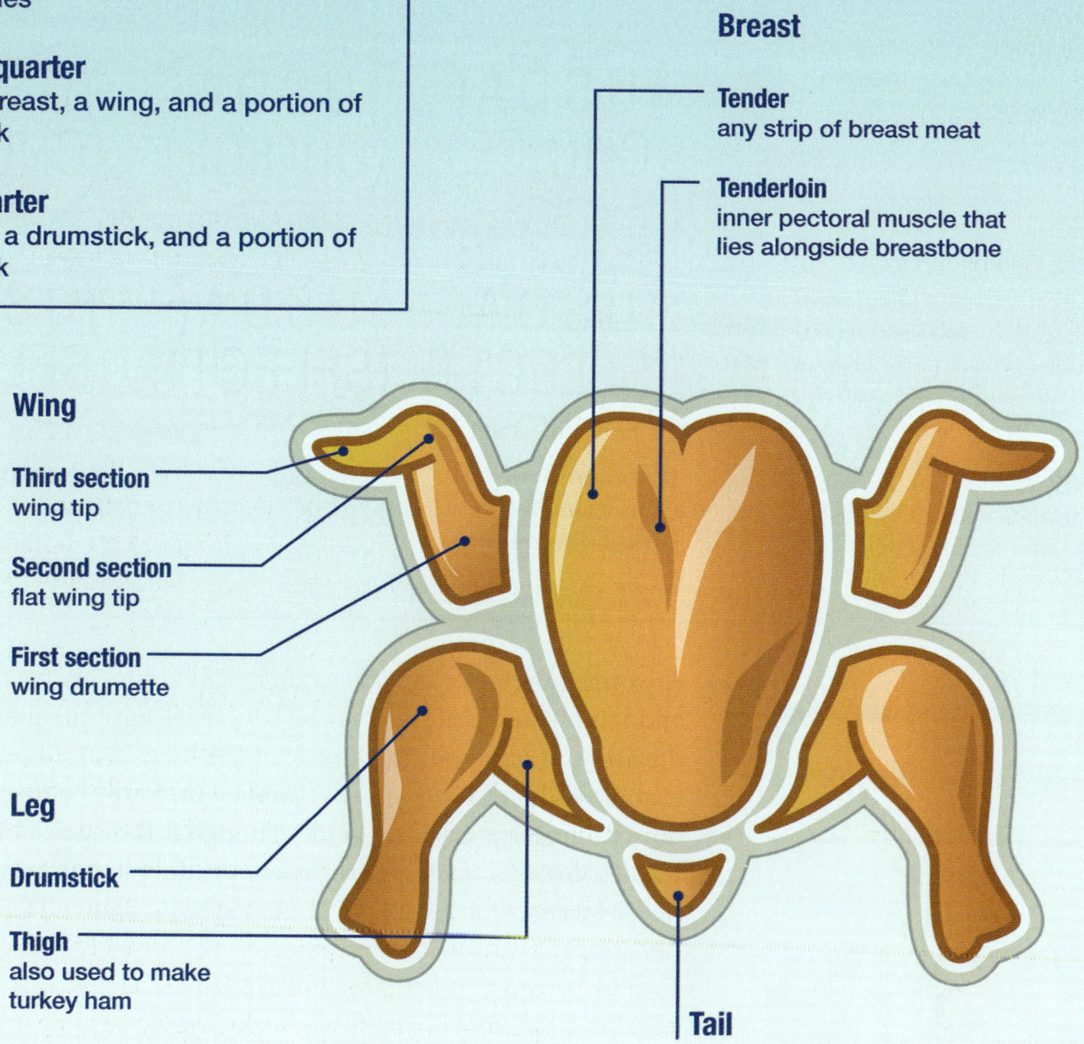

Exhibit 2i

Graded Poultry Parts

- Backs
- Breast quarter
- Breast quarter without wing
- Breasts
- Breasts with ribs
- Drumsticks
- Front poultry halves
- Halves
- Leg quarter
- Legs
- Legs with pelvic bone
- Quarters
- Rear poultry halves
- Tenderloin
- Thighs
- Thighs with back portion
- Wing drumettes
- Wing portions
- Wings
- Wishbones

Choosing the Right Cut

When preparing poultry products, there are two distinct differences depending on the cut chosen: white meat and dark meat. (See *Exhibit 2h.*) Though the difference in color is due to the bird's muscular makeup, each type of meat holds a different nutritive value that makes it stand distinctly apart. **White meat** is found in the areas of the fowl where little muscle use takes place, such as the wings, and as a result is low in calories and fat content. **Dark meat,** on the other hand, is generally located in areas where the bird's muscles are used more heavily, such as the leg and thigh region. While higher in calories and fat, dark meat is usually the meat of preference for consumers seeking a richer, more flavorful meat.

Although they are named for their difference in color, it might be difficult to determine which types of meat are white meat and which are dark meat. While other meat products are white in color, pork, for example, is not considered white meat since it does not hold true to the nutritive makeup that defines white meat found in poultry.

Grades and Class

U.S. grades apply to chicken, turkey, duck, geese, guinea, and pigeon. While all poultry must be inspected, there are no grade standards for poultry parts such as neck, wing tip, tail, and giblets. Quality grades are available for whole poultry, poultry roasts, poultry tenderloins, and poultry parts, including those with or without skin or bone, and fresh or frozen. *Exhibit 2i* provides an approved list of graded poultry parts.

Poultry receives a Grade of A, B, or C based upon a number of guidelines. Poultry must have a good **conformation**—structure and shape—and be free of deformity in the natural form of the product, such as a bent leg or curved backbone. Conditions also taken into account involve flesh, fat covering, defeathering, discolorations, signs of broken or disjointed bones, and freezing defects. Boneless poultry roasts should be free of all bone, cartilage, tendons, visible bruises, and blood clots. **Tenderloin,** a boneless portion of poultry cut from the breast area, is expected to have tendons; however, the tendons must not extend more than one-half inch beyond the meat tissue.

Poultry class provides another distinguishing factor in poultry selection. The class of poultry is defined primarily by the age of the bird. A bird's age generally affects the tenderness, look, and feel of the bird. It also affects the cooking methods necessary to obtain maximum flavor quality. Older birds are less tender than their younger counterparts and are best prepared using moist-heat cooking methods, such as stewing and braising, while more tender, younger birds are suitable for all cooking methods, including barbecuing and frying. See *Exhibit 2j* on the next page for poultry class labels.

Exhibit 2j

Bird Classes

	Chicken	Turkey	Duck	Goose/Guinea	Pigeon
Young	Young chicken, rock cornish hen, broiler, fryer, roaster, capon	Young turkey, fryer-roaster, young hen, young tom	Duckling, young duckling, broiler duckling, fryer duckling, roaster duckling	Young goose/guinea	Squab
Mature	Mature chicken, hen, fowl, baking chicken, stewing chicken	Yearling turkey, mature turkey, old turkey	Mature/old duck	Mature/old goose/guinea	Pigeon

Dairy Products

Milk and products made from milk, such as cheese, yogurt, and butter, are defined as **dairy products.** While some milk is available in raw form, most milk products undergo one or more processes to remove harmful bacteria that may present a health risk. Two processes applied to milk products are pasteurization and homogenization. These processes are defined as follows:

- **Pasteurization**—Process in which milk is heated to kill microorganisms that cause spoilage and disease without diminishing its nutritional value.

- **Homogenization**—Process in which milk is strained through very fine holes to break down fat and blended into one uniform fluid.

Grading Dairy Products

Though dairy products can undergo voluntary inspection and grading to determine quality, this service is used most commonly for products like butter, cheese, and nonfat dry milk. Butter receives one of three U.S. Grades (in order from highest grade to lowest): AA, A, and B, while certain types of cheese receive one of four U.S. Grades: AA, A, B, and C. Other dairy products, such as dry whey, dry buttermilk, or nonfat dry milk, receive approval grades marked with "extra" or "standard." In general, these grades are based upon attributes that are important to the consumer, such as taste, texture, appearance, and color. Dairy products that do not receive grades may still receive a "Quality Approved" rating based on a USDA inspection of the products and facilities. These products are approved for wholesomeness and must satisfy a specific quality level to earn this rating.

The USDA and the Agricultural Marketing Service (AMS) have established U.S. grade standards for four types of cheese:

- Cheddar—Grades AA, A, B, C

- Colby—Grades AA, A, B

- Monterey Jack—Grades AA, A, B

- Swiss and Emmentaler—Grades A, B, C

As with all products stamped with a USDA grade shield, approved dairy products guarantee consistent and dependable quality, with the highest grade representing the best quality standard set by the USDA and lower grades representing products that are wholesome but not ranked as high in terms of quality standards.

Choosing the Right Product

Aside from checking the quality grade for dairy products, choosing the right product is also determined by factors such as the product's intended use, processing needs, nutritional value, and cooking procedures. Because dairy products are taken through a number of processes to remove harmful bacteria, reduce the amount of fat, or add nutritional value and flavor, there is much to consider when choosing the right product.

- **Milk**—Comes in a number of varieties, such as raw milk, whole milk, and lowfat or skim milk. The type of milk you choose is primarily based upon the nutritional qualities you seek. For instance, lactose-intolerant consumers may prefer lactose-reduced milk.

- **Cream**—Contains far more fat than milk. Its use is based primarily on its fat content since that is where its richness comes from. The types of cream that have a larger amount of fat are stable when whipped and add elegance and flavor to many desserts. Whipped cream, for example, contains 30 to 36 percent fat, while coffee cream contains 18 to 30 percent fat.

- **Fermented milk products**—Milk that is fermented has had special bacteria added to produce a healthier product that is high in nutritive value. Examples include buttermilk, sour cream, and yogurt. These items are chosen based upon their flavor and how they are used in food preparation.

- **Butter**—Different types of butter are chosen based upon their flavor attributes and consistency. Available salted and unsalted, butter is used most commonly to add flavor, richness, or smoothness to a dish.

- **Cheese and cheese products.** The flavor characteristics in cheese are influenced by the type of milk used (cow, goat, or sheep), processing, and the method of ripening. (See *Exhibit 2k* on the next page.)

Exhibit 2k

Cheese Varieties

Type of Ripening	Moisture Content	Characteristics	Examples
Fresh, unripened	40–80%	These varieties have a relatively high moisture content. They do not undergo any curing or ripening and should be consumed soon after purchasing.	Cottage cheese, cream cheese, ricotta
Soft, ripened	50–75%	Curing progresses from the outside, or rind, toward the center. Mold and bacterial culture give these varieties their characteristic flavor, body, and texture.	Brie, Camembert, feta
Semisoft, ripened	40–50%	These varieties ripen from the interior, as well as from the surface, with the aid of a mold or bacterial culture.	Bel Paese, Gouda, mozzarella
Blue-veined, mold-ripened	40–50%	Curing is accomplished with bacteria and a characteristic mold culture that grows throughout the interior of these varieties.	Blue (American) or bleu (imported), Gorgonzola, Roquefort
Firm, ripened	30–40%	Ripening occurs from bacterial cultures throughout these varieties. Rate and degree of curing is related to moisture content and usually takes a long time.	Cheddar, Gruyère, Swiss
Very hard, ripened	about 30%	These varieties are cured with a bacterial culture and enzymes. The rate of curing is very slow due to their low moisture and high salt content.	Asiago, Parmesan, Romano

Think About It...

It takes approximately one hundred gallons of milk to produce ten pounds of cheese.

What to Look for in Quality Dry Goods

Dry goods do not have any official USDA grading criteria to measure their levels of quality. Understanding the quality and type of dry goods that appeal to your taste can be determined in a number of alternate ways.

Baking Ingredients

Baking ingredients, such as flour and sugar, are available in different colors, textures, and levels of nutritional value. The differences in quality characteristics among these ingredients will make certain products a better choice for some baking and mixing needs over other products. For example, flours with a higher level of protein are sturdier and will yield heartier and heavier breads than flours with less protein. In contrast, finely ground flours will produce fluffier, lighter breads and pastries.

Flour

There are four common types of flour, as seen in *Exhibit 2l*. The type of flour used in food preparation depends primarily on the products you are baking. However, all-purpose flour can be used for most baking needs. Though many professional bakers may prefer to use flour with one intended purpose, all-purpose flour has a level of **gluten**—a protein found in flour that adds cohesiveness to dough—that allows the baker to create light, fluffy products as well as heavier products.

Exhibit 2l

Flour Varieties

Type	Characteristics	Examples of Use
Bread	Creamy white color; coarse and flaky in texture; high in gluten	Bread, rolls
Cake	Pure white color; fine and smooth in texture; low in gluten	Cake
Pastry	Creamy white color; fine and smooth in texture; gluten level higher than cake flour but lower than bread flour	Cookies, biscuits, muffins
All-purpose	Pure white in color; slightly less gluten than bread flour; used in baking either heavy or light breads and pastries	Most baked goods

Other Flours

Aside from white flour, there are many other flour and meal choices used in baking. **Meal** is a term used for baking products that are not as finely ground as flour, such as cornmeal. Whole-wheat flour is higher in fat and more fragile than white flour, which is why white flour is often used as a substitute or additional ingredient to strengthen breads made from whole-wheat flour. Unlike whole-wheat flour, rye flour does not contain as much gluten, so breads made with rye flour will be heavy. This is also true for breads made with cornmeal, soy flour, and oat flour, unless other ingredients are added to make up for the lack of gluten.

Sugar

Consumers will generally classify sugar as a sweetening agent used to enhance the flavor of food and beverages. Sugar is also used as a preservative, to create toppings such as meringue, and to soften the texture of baked goods by breaking down gluten structure.

Classified by the texture of its grains, sugar is broken down into two major categories: granulated sugar and confectioners' or powdered sugar.

■ **Granulated sugar,** also called table sugar, is sugar in the form of small granules. Available in three textures, from very coarse to very fine, granulated sugar is the most commonly used form of sugar. With the ability to support higher quantities of fat, these types of sugar are most often used to bake cakes and cookies.

■ **Confectioners' sugar,** also referred to as powdered sugar, is ground into a fine powder and mixed with starch to avoid lumping. This type of sugar is also available in a variety of textures. These types of sugar are most commonly used to make icings, toppings, and cream fillings.

With such a wide array of selections, there is sure to be a specific sugar that meets your needs. Whether you are seeking to create a light, fluffy icing or doughnuts, choosing the right sugar is based primarily on its texture. The finer the sugar, the lighter the baked item will be. Coarser sugar holds better and works best with fat to create various items. (See *Exhibit 2m.*)

Exhibit 2m

Sugar Varieties

Type	Characteristics	Uses
Granulated Sugars		
Sanding sugar	Coarsest grains	Sprinkled on doughnuts, cakes, cookies
Regular table sugar	Small grains	Used for home baking, coffee/tea
Very fine, ultrafine	Ground from table sugar, very fine grains	Cakes and cookies have uniform batter
Confectioners' or Powdered Sugars		
XX and 4X	Coarsest powdered	Dusting on pastries
6X	Standard powdered	Icings, toppings
10X	Smoothest texture	Icings

Other Sweeteners

Food can also be sweetened using brown sugar or chocolate. **Brown sugar** is an ingredient derived from mixing refined sugar with molasses. Its brown color is attributed to the amount of molasses added; dark brown sugar has a higher quantity of molasses and a richer flavor than light brown sugar. Brown sugar will stay softer longer than white sugar and is best used in baked goods that should have a softer feel, such as oatmeal raisin cookies.

Chocolate is produced from dry cocoa powder that has been processed from fermented, roasted, and ground cocoa beans. Dry cocoa powder, cocoa butter, sugar, milk, and other flavorings are blended together to create the unique taste of chocolate. Chocolate is then **tempered,** which means it undergoes a heating and cooling process for stabilization to make the chocolate smooth and shiny. With three bean varieties used interchangeably to make chocolate, the type of bean(s) used will affect the flavor of the chocolate; the roasting process and the level of cocoa butter and cocoa solids will also influence the taste of the chocolate. (See *Exhibit 2n.*)

Exhibit 2n

Chocolate Varieties

Type	Composition
Unsweetened or baking	About 53 percent cocoa butter and 47 percent cocoa solids. No sugar added; not suitable for eating.
Bittersweet	Minimal amounts of sugar; at least 35 percent chocolate liquor
Semisweet	Moderate amount of sugar; 15 to 35 percent chocolate liquor
Milk chocolate	Contains milk and sugar. Typically used for eating; tends to burn if used in baking.
Couverture	At least 32 percent cocoa butter. Can be used to make thin, shiny coating for pastries. Usually of very high quality and expensive.

Exhibit 2o

Every baker must understand how ingredients work together in order to produce the best baked goods.

Leavening Ingredients

Leavening is the process in which baked products produce gases that cause dough to rise during preparation or baking. Leavening ingredients must be handled with care because subtle changes or handling procedures can cause major defects in the baked product. (See *Exhibit 2o.*) Examples of leavening ingredients include yeast, baking soda, and baking powder.

Yeast

Yeast is a living organism that is used in beer and bread production. When combined with sugar and water, yeast produces carbon dioxide and alcohol; this process is called **fermentation.** The gas produced causes leavening in baked products. Yeast begins to rise once activated, either through blending or mixing fresh yeast with other ingredients, then adding water; or by adding warm water between 105°F to 115°F (41°C to 46°C) to dry yeast.

Dry yeast is one of two main yeasts used in baking. The other is fresh yeast. Compressed **fresh yeast,** or wet yeast, works faster and longer than dry yeast; however, fresh yeast is highly perishable and loses its potency a few weeks after it is packed. Preferred for its flavor, fresh yeast is typically pale beige in color, crumbly, and compressed with a sweet, fruity smell. Available in regular or quick-rising forms, active **dry yeast** has grown to be a popular choice, favored for its longer shelf life and higher tolerance for handling. An unopened package of quick-rising yeast has a shelf life of two years, whereas a freezer-kept batch of fresh yeast will last up to four months. Without freezing, fresh yeast has only a one- or two-week life span.

In most cases, choosing the yeast that fits your needs is a matter of preference. Many professional bakers view fresh yeast as superior, and they will give credit to this ingredient for their flavorful breads. While some consumers might be able to successfully use fresh yeast within its short life span, others find that dry yeast works just as well with less effort. All types of yeast are relatively fragile and must be carefully handled and maintained within specific temperatures to retain potency. Therefore, choosing the right yeast depends greatly on the handling method and storage conditions associated with its use.

Think About It...

Because yeast is a live organism, you should always check the expiration date on the package before using to ensure that it is still active.

Baking Soda

Baking soda can be used as a leavening agent on its own in recipes where an acid ingredient is present. The combination of moisture and acid releases carbon dioxide that leavens baked products. Unlike yeast, baking soda does not need to be prepared in warmer temperatures in order for a leavening effect to take place. Therefore, baked products prepared with baking soda must be baked at once, before the gases escape and become inactive. The leavening power is based upon the quantity of baking soda used, although too much baking soda will affect the flavor of the baked product. Examples of acids that react with baking soda are honey, molasses, cocoa, and buttermilk.

Baking Powder

More versatile than baking soda, baking powder is created from a mixture of baking soda, for its leavening power; acid, to activate the baking soda once moistened; and starch, to keep the baking powder from absorbing moisture prematurely. One form of baking powder is single-acting baking powder, which reacts immediately to moisture, as baking soda does, and requires speedy preparation to preserve its leavening power during baking. Baking powder is also available as double-acting baking powder, which has an immediate leavening reaction to moisture and a more robust leavening reaction once heated. Double-acting baking powder allows batter to be held for a longer period of time before baking.

Oils, Vinegars, and Other Cooking Liquids

Whether you intend to add flavor to a dish or tone down its spiciness, oils, vinegars, and wines can be key ingredients that set your recipes apart from others.

Cooking Oils and Fat

Cooking oils are purified liquid fat derived from seeds, nuts, or vegetables. Among the most popular types are canola, olive, corn, soybean, and peanut. While the range of oil types varies greatly, an oil is often chosen based upon taste, nutritional qualities, processing, and—as always—its intended use.

In many cases, oil is extracted by applying pressure to seeds, nuts, or vegetables. The extracted oil is then refined. The process of refining oil consists of numerous processes that remove impurities resulting in colorless, odorless oil without much of its natural flavor. Refined oils, such as vegetable oil, can be cooked at higher temperatures without burning and smoking. Oil is also available unrefined. Unrefined oils are lightly filtered to remove some impurities, but not so many that the oil loses its natural color, aroma, and flavor. Some unrefined oils, such as virgin olive oil—produced from the first of two pressings of the olives—are greater in flavor and nutritional value than refined oils.

Oils may undergo further processing that will change their liquid form into a solid fat suitable for other purposes. For example, oil can be **hydrogenated,** which means that hydrogen is added so it remains solid at room temperature. This process produces **shortening.** Shortening incorporates tenderness into food and is often used in baking or deep-frying. **Margarine** is also a solid fat and is produced from hydrogenated oil with vegetable or animal fat added. Margarine may be used as a substitute for shortening, though it tends to leave a more butter-like flavor in the finished dish.

Vinegars

Vinegar is used as a preservative in pickles and chutneys; it is also an ingredient in marinades and salad dressings. Made by acetic fermentation, a process that converts alcohol to acid, a small amount of good quality vinegar can lift the flavor of many cooked meat and poultry dishes. The selection and production of vinegar is based upon the wine, sherry, beer, or cider used to produce its flavor and the aging process used. While most countries produce their own type of vinegar, the laws that govern the origin of a particular vinegar also strictly control its production.

Quality vinegar, like wine, is aged for years before consumption. Vinegars range in age from a younger vinegar of three to five years' maturation to a much older and highly prized vinegar of twelve years and up to 150 years. Balsamic vinegar, for instance, is made from white grape juice and fermented for four to twenty-plus years to produce its intensely rich, concentrated flavor.

Cooking with Alcohol and Wine

Think About It...

If you do not enjoy the taste of a particular wine in a glass, chances are that you will not enjoy its taste in your food.

Wine, sherry, brandy, Madeira, and other forms of alcohol are used to intensify the flavor of sauces, soups, braised food, desserts, and a number of different entrées. Wines are **reduced**—boiled or flamed to reduce the strength of the alcohol content. Dishes that contain reduced wines have less than half the amount of alcohol of the wine used in them. Additionally, dishes prepared with wines that have not been properly reduced may have an unpleasant taste when cooked.

Wines are available in such a variety of colors, tastes, and qualities that the choices may seem endless. Using good quality, young, and powerful wines to maximize the quality of your dish may be difficult but not impossible. Following are a number of pointers that will help you in wine selection:

- **Premium does not always mean better.** Because it takes time for the flavor attributes of a particular wine to develop during preparation, it is important to use a wine that can withstand the high temperature and duration of cooking necessary to deliver its full flavor impact. Premium wines require careful handling and cooking conditions that will not allow this process to easily happen. Wines that are generally of good quality will hold better in higher temperatures and last longer throughout cooking. Save the premium wine and serve it with the dish.

- **Choose by taste.** Though the quality of the dish often depends on the quality of the wine chosen, purchasing an expensive wine is not always the answer. Choose the taste you feel would best complement your dish. It is the wine's fruity, sour, or sweet flavor that will have a direct effect on the flavor of the dish.

■ **Keep it simple.** Cooking with wine requires careful selection. Select a wine based upon the taste, quality, and resilience necessary to satisfy your production needs.

You may find that some wines have packaging that says "cooking wine" or "cooking sherry." The labels on these wines show that preservatives have been added, commonly salt, and are of satisfactory quality for cooking. These wines, however, are salty and are not suitable for drinking. The salty flavor of a cooking wine will have a different effect on a dish than a regular drinking wine.

Wines used when preparing a recipe should be specific to the wine listed. Substituting a wine may result in a dish that has substandard quality by comparison. *Exhibit 2p* shows how wines are paired with dishes in cooking.

Exhibit 2p

Using Wine in Cooking

Type of Wine	Type of Food
Red wine	■ Dishes with red meat (beef, veal, lamb, etc.) ■ Red-colored savory sauces ■ Soup with vegetables or beef
White wine	■ Dishes with white meat, seafood, or pork ■ Seafood stews
Sweet wine	■ Desserts

Herbs and Spices

Herbs and spices, though considered synonymous by some, are different ingredients used to flavor food. Spices are derived from the seeds or bark of aromatic, fragrant plants grown in tropical climates; some examples are ginger, paprika, nutmeg, and cinnamon. Culinary herbs, available fresh or dried, come from leafy, green plants, such as sage, parsley, and basil, grown in temperate climates.

Since "herbs and spices" has become an all-inclusive term used to describe a wide range of flavoring blends, it is important to use these flavorings skillfully. To do this, you must become familiar with the herbs and spices you are using. A quick and easy way to do this would be to taste each on its own. That way, when you taste the dishes you plan to serve, you will be able to identify the flavoring that would be just right for the flavor enhancement you need. Experiment with quantities to ensure that the right amount is added so as not to overpower the dish.

Activity

Choosing the Right Flavorings

Select two herbs and two spices. For each herb and spice, list an entrée and another dish (soup, salad, accompaniment, or dessert) in which you would use the herb or spice. *Note:* You would not necessarily serve the entrée and other dish in the same meal.

Herb or Spice	Entrée	Other dish
Herb **1**:		
Herb **2**:		
Spice **1**:		
Spice **2**:		

What quality considerations do you need to keep in mind when choosing which herbs and spices to use?

_____

_____

_____

Quality of Canned Goods

Since you can find just about any edible product in a can these days, it is important to consider a number of factors before purchasing and using canned goods. Canned goods have an indefinite life span as long as the can is not opened or severely damaged. Cans that appear to be swollen should be avoided because swelling is a common effect of spoilage. Though many canned goods are nutritious, their quality differs based upon the flavor and appearance of the food. You must consider whether the canned good you select will produce the desired quality you seek in a finished dish.

Canned items, such as vegetables, are often graded for wholesomeness. U.S. Grades A, B, and C are given to canned vegetables based upon their color, tenderness, flavor, and appearance. As a result, higher-grade canned vegetables would have better taste and appearance, whereas lower-grade canned vegetables would not be as uniform in color and flavor but would be acceptable as an ingredient in soups or casseroles. Graded canned goods are inspected throughout the packaging process and require specific labeling to be placed on the can that indicates the product's net weight, common name and style, and the liquid in which the product has been packaged.

Ethnic Food Products

Ethnic food products represent the dishes that are traditionally cooked and served in other countries around the world. These products are commonly based on characteristic spices, ingredients, cooking methods, and flavors found in the dishes served in a particular culture. The key to creating quality ethnic dishes is to choose the signature food ingredients necessary for the final dish to taste authentic. Consider making your marinara sauce or guacamole from scratch instead of buying a ready-to-use package. Purchasing ingredients from an ethnic food supplier may also increase the ethnic flavor characteristic of your finished dish. Selecting the best items for these types of cuisine starts with identifying the attributes found in a particular ethnic food. For example, some ethnic dishes may contain ingredients than might be spicier, saltier, or milder than the ingredients used in other dishes. Becoming knowledgeable about these differences will help determine the ingredients you choose.

Understanding Proper Receiving Conditions and Foodhandling

Although inspection and grading procedures are implemented to minimize the likelihood of contamination in food products, contamination can still occur with improper handling procedures during preparation. To alleviate the probability of this occurrence, the USDA requires concise safe handling and cooking procedures to be placed on raw poultry and meat items. **Value-added** or processed products do not require such labeling.

Advanced Methods of Packaging

There are several methods, in addition to refrigeration, to preserve the shelf life of food products beyond that of standard refrigeration, canning, or dehydration. There are also more advanced processes, some of which are shown in *Exhibit 2q* on the next page.

Exhibit 2q

Methods of Food Packaging

Method	Description
Modified atmosphere packaging (MAP)	MAP is a process in which air is vacuumed out of a food package and replaced with gases, such as carbon dioxide and nitrogen. Many fresh-cut produce items are packaged in this way.
Sous vide	Food is vacuum-packed in individual pouches, partially or fully cooked, and then chilled. This food is then heated for service in the establishment. Some frozen, precooked meals are packaged in this way.
Ultra-high temperature (UHT)	UHT food is heat-treated at very high temperatures (pasteurized) for a short time to kill microorganisms. These items are often also aseptically packaged—sealed under sterile conditions to keep them from being contaminated. Individual packages of cream for coffee are one example.

Summary

"Know your product" is a phrase you will continue to hear as you learn about the restaurant and foodservice industry. Knowing the way a product can be used—and abused—is a powerful tool in successfully producing quality food.

Food products should be chosen to meet standards based on a number of factors, such as their intended use, method of preparation, or nutritional value. Food selection can also be determined based upon inspections that assess products for safety and wholesomeness. These products receive stamps of approval upon satisfying specific qualifications.

In addition to mandated food inspections, food products may also receive quality grades and, in some cases, yield grades. Understanding quality grades and what they mean in relation to the products that you serve can improve your selection process and help you to choose the right products, and their substitutes, every time.

Food products and ingredients are available in many varieties to serve a vast number of needs in food preparation. Being able to identify the quality attributes of seafood, meat, poultry, dairy products, and dry goods will aid you in setting the standards used in your recipes and operation.

Review Your Learning

1 Which is *not* inspected by the USDA?

A. Meat

B. Vegetables

C. Dry goods

D. Fruits

2 The chef wants to ensure dark meat is used in his stew. What section of the chicken should *not* be cut?

A. Breast

B. Leg

C. Thigh

D. Drumstick

3 Poultry is graded according to which system?

A. USDA 1, USDA 2, USDA 3

B. U.S. Grade A, U.S. Grade B, U.S. Grade C

C. Prime, Select, Choice, Utility

D. Grade AA, Grade A, Grade B, Grade Extra

4 What is the highest grade given to cheese by the USDA?

A. USDA Excellent

B. USDA No. 1

C. USDA AAA

D. USDA Grade AA Cheese

5 Which part of poultry does *not* receive a quality grade?

A. Tenderloins

B. Giblets

C. Whole poultry

D. Poultry roast

6 A canned good should *not* be purchased if the

A. can is swollen.

B. canned good does not have a quality grade.

C. canned product is held in oil.

D. product is not uniform in color.

7 What is the best way to learn more about a particular ethnic cuisine?

A. Order all the ethnic products that are available from your vendor.

B. Learn to speak the language of the culture from which the food derives.

C. Only hire chefs of the same culture.

D. Purchase signature food ingredients from an ethnic food supplier.

8 What happens if the wine in your dish is *not* properly reduced before serving?

A. The food will be too soupy.

B. Consumers will become intoxicated.

C. The food will have a strong alcohol taste.

D. The food will spoil.

Notes

Receiving and Storing to Maintain Quality

3

After completing this chapter, you should be able to:

- Describe how an establishment communicates with vendors about its receiving and storing requirements.
- Describe receiving procedures that relate to food quality.
- Describe storing procedures that relate to food quality.

Test Your Knowledge

1. **True or False:** Vendors must have quality certifications. *(See p. 49.)*

2. **True or False:** All staff can check in deliveries. *(See p. 52.)*

3. **True or False:** There are special areas for each type of vegetable in a cooler. *(See p. 65.)*

4. **True or False:** The FIFO system ensures that the newest product is used first. *(See p. 49.)*

5. **True or False:** Canned goods do not spoil. *(See p. 68.)*

Key Terms

Ethylene gas	Oxidation
First in, first out (FIFO)	Perpetual inventory
Flash freezing	Supplier list

Introduction

Food quality depends not only on finding the perfect quality food from the best vendor, but also on having the food delivered and available in your establishment when you are ready to use it.

You must have procedures in place to receive and store food properly. You must know the shelf life of both perishable and nonperishable food to maximize your storage space. You must also have procedures in place to use food in an order that maintains its quality. Storing food properly is a critical task. A great deal of food is lost due to improper storage. Consider your establishment's receiving and storage facilities, and communicate these to your vendors so they know of any special requirements.

Building a System That Maintains Product Quality

All restaurant and foodservice establishments should have a system in place for receiving and storing food. This means having a strategy to ensure that receiving and storage is orderly, problems can be fixed when needed, inventory is taken regularly, and a regular review of the way vendors and staff perform is done.

There are numerous considerations about your establishment that affect receiving and storage when working with vendors. You need to explain to vendors any considerations specific to your establishment that may affect receiving and storage. Explaining your requirements to the vendor makes it easier for you to work with them and reduces the amount of food you will need to discard or return because it does not match and/or meet your facility's requirements. Planning to check on stored food on a regular basis, both perishable and nonperishable items, will save you money in the long run. Using the **first-in, first-out** system, usually referred to as **FIFO,** assures that older products are used before newer products so that the first items placed in storage are the first to be taken out and used.

Supplier Selection Criteria

Prior to ordering, receiving, and storing quality products, you must consider where the products were grown or produced. The best receiving and storing policies and procedures cannot make a poor quality product better once you have it in your establishment. Thus, choosing a creditable supplier is key. Those with purchasing responsibility should seek suppliers who are considered to be ethical, reliable, and financially stable or deemed to be part of the approved **supplier list**. This is a list of suppliers who have met the operation's criteria in regard to food safety, product quality, and price. In regards to food safety, the FDA defines "approved" as acceptable to the regulatory authority based on a determination of conformity with principles, practices, and generally recognized standards that protect public health.

Once a supplier has met the above criteria, the process is not over. You must closely examine the supplier's practices. In some instances, vendors outsource the supply of certain products to another vendor or outsource their delivery to a third party service. In either case, you have to make sure that these additional parties meet your criteria and will supply you with the same desired results.

Here are points to verify when you select a supplier:

- Vendors who supply meat, poultry, and egg products must be inspected by the USDA. (See *Exhibit 3a.*)

- Vendors must be compliant with applicable local, state, and federal law.

- Vendors should be able to supply a list of references to prove they are reputable.

Exhibit 3a

Poultry products must be inspected by the USDA.

■ Vendors that are inspected must have a Hazard Analysis and Critical Control Point (HACCP) program in place.

■ Vendors that provide refrigerated or frozen products must have holding units that can maintain the product at the required internal temperature.

■ Vendor delivery trucks must be able to maintain the required product temperature.

■ Vendors must have practices and procedures in place to ensure that their personnel are following proper personal hygiene practices.

Supplier Contract

Once you select a supplier, put a contract in place. Points to review with the vendor and to include in the contract include:

■ Ask the supplier to visit your establishment to take notes about anything that could make the delivery process difficult. Review the receiving area together, viewing the amount of room, exits, doors, etc.

■ Discuss acceptable delivery times and days.

■ Communicate with the vendor your requirements for the drop-off area (e.g., how long a vendor's truck may be in an unrefrigerated area). You also need to know whether the vendor's truck is loaded in a refrigerated area. If not, the loading time adds additional exposure for the food to be time-temperature abused, which can make food unsafe.

■ Specify in the contract who can accept a delivery.

■ Be sure to communicate your standards to the vendor in writing, when possible.

Evaluate Suppliers

At least once per year, review the performance of your vendors. Take notes about issues that arise and how the vendor resolved them. At the yearly review, determine whether the service, quality of products, and prices meet your standards. Meet with the vendors and review any issues. If you decide to renew your contract, review it again before signing.

Receiving Requirements for Quality

Choosing a reputable and reliable supplier is the first step in receiving and storing food to maintain quality. The next step is to have receiving policies and procedures that will ensure that as well.

A great deal of the receiving process involves working with people—suppliers and staff—to ensure that the food received meets your standards and then is handled properly. As the manager, it is your responsibility to make sure that the food leaves the supplier's facility safely and remains safe until it is safely secured in your establishment. You have to specify to your supplier what your expectations are in regards to delivering products to you.

Deliveries

Receiving food must be done quickly and efficiently to preserve the quality of the food; therefore it is very important to select a time with your vendor at which you can give the attention needed to receive the delivery correctly. Deliveries should be designated to times when the operation is slow. You do not want your staff to worry about receiving and putting away products at the same time they are servicing customers. Proper delivery timing can only be accomplished by establishing a good relationship with your vendors, so you can count on them consistently to deliver food to your requirements. Food safety must be a high priority in your receiving process and cannot be compromised by any means. This requires that you have procedures in place so that your staff can inspect food, reject it if necessary, quickly unload it, and transfer it to the storage area.

A typical independent food establishment may work with multiple vendors, each delivering its own specialty. There may be separate vendors for seafood, meat, poultry, produce, and breads. (See *Exhibit 3b.*) Your establishment should have quality standards and receiving criteria in place for each vendor that delivers product to your operation. In addition to the vendors meeting your quality

Exhibit 3b

An operation typically uses several specialty vendors.

requirements, it is imperative that they meet your required delivery times as well. Having them arrive and unload in a timely manner is important.

For example, if deliveries are scheduled every Monday, Wednesday, and Friday, during a two-hour window of 5 a.m. to 7 a.m., and four suppliers scheduled to arrive at thirty-minute intervals, it is critical that they are on time and quickly unload your product. You do not want a log jam of suppliers at your back door because this potentially could jeopardize the safety and quality of the product being delivered.

Signing for Deliveries

Only allow a staff member at an intermediate or advanced level to sign for deliveries. (See *Exhibit 3c*.) This person also needs to have the authority to move the food to the proper areas.

Signing rights can affect quality. If you allow anyone in the establishment to receive and sign for deliveries, no one will be responsible for the quality of the received food. Put a person in charge of the receiving function who has extensive product and menu knowledge. This person will reject unacceptable food, which saves money and maintains quality. In most instances, the manager has the responsibility to sign for deliveries as well.

Consider Frequency of Deliveries

The frequency of deliveries can help preserve food quality. Some food must be delivered daily, while other food can safely be delivered weekly. You need to weigh the advantage of daily and weekly deliveries for freshness against the added time that receiving takes.

- **Fish**—Fresh fish should be delivered daily, frozen fish perhaps only weekly.

- **Produce**—Certain fresh produce should be delivered daily, bulk and hardy vegetables weekly.

- **Specialty produce**—Delicate or specialty produce, such as wild mushrooms, mesclun mix lettuce, and tropical fruit (mangoes, kumquats) with a short shelf life, should be ordered daily according to its specifications sheet.

   There are specialty products that are shelf stable and do not need to be ordered daily. There is a financial advantage to bulk ordering some specialty sauces or specialty items for the pastry department, such as chocolates, flours, and decorations.

Exhibit 3c

The staff member who signs for deliveries is responsible for the quality of the received items.

- **Meat**—Regardless if dry or wet aged, meat should be ordered and delivered at least two or three times a week. This will depend mostly on the establishment's usage and storage capacity.

- **Dairy**—Dairy product should be ordered at least twice a week. Milk and eggs have a good shelf life, but you should not stretch the time too far. Cheeses are very shelf stable as long as they are kept in the cooler.

Advantages of Weekly Deliveries

The menu that you offer and the type of operation you run will strongly influence whether you have deliveries come weekly or daily. For example, if your restaurant has seafood as its only option with an average price per entrée of $25.00, then a customer's expectation might be that all fish served has been received and prepared that day. Whereas, if you are a casual-dining operation with an eclectic menu, and fish is one of many options, then the customer's expectation might not be that the fish is fresh. Frozen fish that is delivered weekly might be acceptable in that situation. There are advantages to weekly deliveries:

- Price breaks on quantity purchases

- Receiving staff or a steward/clerk only needed once a week; money saved if staff do not need to be available daily

Receiving Procedures

Well-defined receiving procedures ensure that an operation receives only the products that meet its established standards for quality and quantity and rejects product that does not meet these standards. The operation's manager has the responsibility for establishing appropriate procedures for receiving and putting away food, training the designated staff members in these procedures, and monitoring the receiving function. Implementing appropriate procedures helps to prevent product deterioration that can lead to spoiled food and a higher food cost for the operation. Appropriate procedures include provisions for:

- Accepting or rejecting delivered food

- Putting food away

- Maintaining the cleanliness and safety of the receiving area

Procedure for Accepting or Rejecting Food

When a supplier delivers its products, the designated staff member of the receiving operation (receiving clerk) must check the delivery while the delivery person is on the premises. The receiving clerk must check each product against the delivery invoice and the purchase order to ensure that all ordered products were received and that each product matches the desired quality standards. In addition, the receiving clerk is responsible for ensuring that the quantity received matches the quantity ordered. The receiving clerk must be sure that large boxes, especially of meat, contain the number and specification ordered. For example, if a box of twenty-four, 12-ounce steaks was ordered, then all twenty-four must each weigh 12 ounces. Disreputable suppliers have been known to substitute some 10-ounce steaks for 12-ounce steaks—but they put the smaller steaks between the correctly sized steaks.

If product does not meet the established quality and quantity standards, it must be rejected. Accepting inferior product wastes the operation's money and prevents the operation from meeting its quality standards and the standards of its customers. When the receiving clerk notices unacceptable food, he or she should do the following:

Exhibit 3d

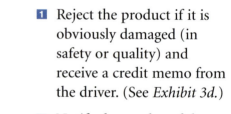

Product that is damaged or does not meet safety or quality standards must be rejected.

1 Reject the product if it is obviously damaged (in safety or quality) and receive a credit memo from the driver. (See *Exhibit 3d.*)

2 Notify the vendor of the situation. The vendor should immediately send a substitute for the damaged product.

3 Note the rejected product on the purchase order and invoice.

4 Notify the manager of the restaurant or foodservice operation.

5 Tell the manager when this situation is resolved.

Once food has been accepted, staff must be notified so they can put it away. In most operations the person who signs for the delivery is also responsible for placing the food into storage.

Put Food Away Promptly

Putting food away promptly preserves food quality and, therefore, money. Meat, fish, poultry, and dairy are subject to time-temperature abuse. Frozen food can defrost, and cold products can rise to unsafe temperatures. If food becomes unsafe, it must be discarded. If unsafe food is served, there is a danger of customers getting sick.

Fresh and Frozen Products

When food has been accepted, take care with fresh food items. Fresh and frozen food must be put away as soon as possible. If food items are kept on ice, allow for water/ice to drain properly.

- **Frozen food** cannot wait. Do not let frozen food defrost. If food is allowed to defrost, the quality of the product will decrease.

- **Fresh fish, fresh meat, poultry, and all dairy products** should first be checked for quality, safety, and compliance with order specifications. Food must be transferred immediately to the cooling area.

- **Produce** can be put away last, especially items that do not require refrigeration.

Seafood

You should be especially careful of receiving seafood because temperature abuse is a serious quality and safety problem during this time. Here are the quality-check guidelines to follow when you receive any fresh fish:

- Fresh fish must be received at 41°F (5°C) or lower and should be surrounded by crushed, self-draining ice.

- Fresh fish should have a mild ocean or seaweed smell.

- Both eyes of the fish should be bright, clear, and full.

- The gills should be bright red.

- The skin of the fish should be shiny, brightly colored, and clean.

- The meat should not show indentations after you press it with your finger.

Shellfish at Delivery: Live and Refrigerated and Frozen

There are guidelines for the condition of shellfish, whether live or refrigerated or frozen at delivery, as shown in *Exhibit 3e* on the next page.

Exhibit 3e

Shellfish Receiving Guide

Product	Live Shellfish	Refrigerated and Frozen Shellfish
Bivalves (such as mussels, clams, scallops)	Certain live bivalves can be open or closed at receiving, but have to close when tapped. Tapping does not apply to oysters. **Important:** If bivalves stay closed after cooking, they are not safe to eat and should be discarded.	Shellfish should arrive refrigerated at 41°F (5°C) or lower or frozen shucked in their own juice, or frozen packaged single shell (half shell).
Oysters	Oysters have to be closed at arrival. If there is a strong smell of ammonia, they should be rejected.	Shucked oysters should arrive in a plastic container in their own juice.
Lobster/Crab	Lobster has to be moving on arrival.	Frozen lobsters should be cooked from the frozen stage because of possible spoilage during defrosting and cannot be sold as fresh.
Crayfish/ Shrimp, etc.	Seldom bought live. If purchased live, same procedures as live lobster.	Usually comes frozen in specific counts, size, and weight of individual shrimp. For example, sixteen to twenty shrimp in a pound means each shrimp about 1 ounce to 1⅛ ounce in size.

Fresh Meat

When checking in fresh meat, be sure to measure the temperature of vacuum-sealed, portion-cut steaks for correct temperature. You can place the thermometer between two sealed packages. You do not need to stick the thermometer through the plastic or unwrap any meat cuts.

Produce

Fresh produce is fairly safe for quite awhile in a clean environment. Not all vegetables and fruit need to be cooled. Examples of vegetables that should not be stored in refrigeration are potatoes, onions, garlic, and tomatoes. (Other produce storage requirements will be discussed in the storage segment.)

Nonperishable Goods

Nonperishable goods are usually purchased from a general supplier who sometimes sells more than just food products, such as paper goods and disposable products.

Nonperishable goods may have expiration dates, but most have a packaging date, which is when it was packaged. A guideline for purchasing nonperishable or dry goods is that you should always have in your storage 1.5 times the amount you will need on your busiest production day.

Exhibit 3f

Various Types of Storage Areas

Freezer

Cooler

Dry storage

Live shellfish tank

Maintain the Receiving Area

The receiving area should be an environment that will not diminish the quality of the product and its safety. Obviously, the area must be clean. Follow these ideas to keep the receiving area clean and safe:

- Area must be well lit.

- Area must be free of pests and rodents (when doors are open during delivery, animals can enter quickly).

- Area must be easy to clean; staff must be able to clean up spills quickly and easily.

- Floors must be nonslip to prevent accidents due to spilled ice and delivery moisture. Usually the icemaker is close to this area—do not allow the icemaker to overflow.

Storage Procedures That Relate to Food Quality

Storing food properly is one of the most important tasks you have as a foodservice professional. Perishable food must obviously be monitored daily to preserve its quality. You need to know the characteristics of the storage areas in your operation, as well as the shelf life of the perishable ingredients being stored. You also need to know how to plan and maintain an inventory system.

Storage Areas in a Food Establishment

In a restaurant or foodservice establishment, you will find different storage areas for different needs to keep the highest possible quality during storage for your food items. (See *Exhibit 3f.*) Air circulation in any storage area is critical to keep food cool or frozen, or to prevent food from getting moldy. Following is a list of the different storage areas and their optimal use:

- **Freezers**—Must be at 0°F (−18°C) or below. Freezers are usually either walk-in or have front door or trunk openings. Most commonly you will find a walk-in freezer holding speed racks, or shelving, to provide enough space for items to have enough room to freeze properly. Air movement is crucial in both the freezer and cooler. Clean a freezer at least once a week. The floors are only washable with antifreeze or salted hot water.

- **Coolers**—Must be able to hold food at 41°F (5°C) or lower. Coolers and freezers have a fan blowing the cold air around in the room. Again, it is very important to keep the air moving between products. Avoid placing product on sheet pans, since this hampers air circulation. The cooler should be monitored on a daily basis to ensure cleanliness.

Freezers and coolers must be tested for the correct temperature regularly. Establishments with a HACCP program may test freezer and cooler temperatures every two hours or at least twice a day.

- **Dry storage**—Moisture and heat are the biggest dangers to dry and canned food. The temperature of the storeroom should be between 50°F and 70°F (10°C and 21°C). Keep relative humidity at 50 to 60 percent, if possible. All shelving in any of the areas must be at least six inches off the ground. This space is necessary to make access for rodents difficult and to provide enough space to clean underneath the shelving on a daily basis.

- **Live shellfish tanks**—Not many establishments will have the luxury to have a live shellfish tank for their fresh crabs, lobsters, etc. If your establishment decides to display shellfish in a tank prior to service, you may do so under two conditions:

  □ The tanks carry a sign stating that the shellfish are for display only.

  □ You obtain a variance from the local health department.

Rotating and Storing Product

Food must be stored with proper labels, while all products in storage must be rotated following the FIFO system. Managers must also regularly inventory all products.

Labeling

Restaurant and foodservice establishments often purchase adhesive labels that are color-coded to track daily prepared food, such as gravy or deli meats, or for products that are premeasured for the line, such as portioned pasta, cheeses, or portion-cut meats and vegetables.

Some establishments use seven colored dots, one for each day of the week. The labels must be waterproof, and you must use permanent markers so dates can be written and read easily. You must decide whether the labels designate the last-use date or the date food was prepared. Or, as shown in *Exhibit 3g*, you can indicate both the prepared date and the use-by date on the same label. If you choose to put only one date on the label, then all staff must know what the date represents.

A common practice used in dry storage is to place items alphabetically from the top left corner to the bottom right. This helps track items and makes taking inventory easier.

Exhibit 3g

Examples of Labels

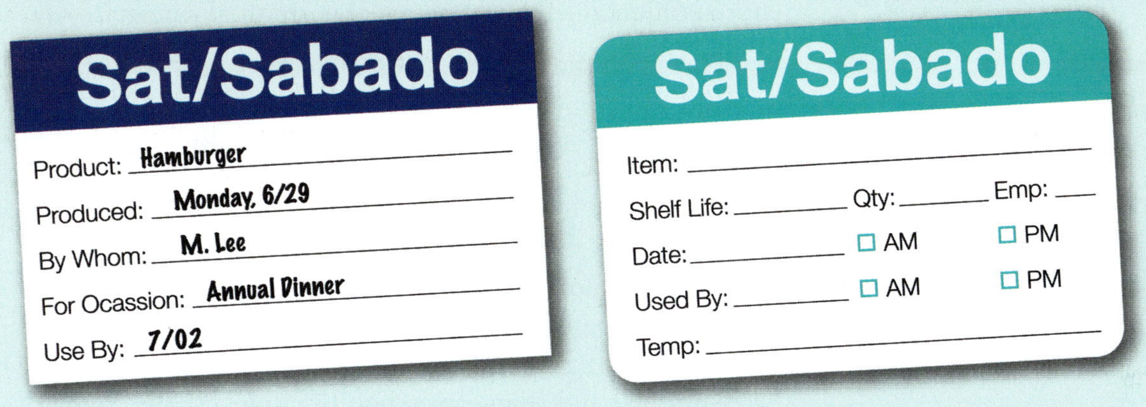

Sat/Sabado

Product: __Hamburger__

Produced: __Monday, 6/29__

By Whom: __M. Lee__

For Ocassion: __Annual Dinner__

Use By: __7/02__

Sat/Sabado

Item: _____

Shelf Life: _____ Qty: _____ Emp: _____

Date: _____ ☐ AM ☐ PM

Used By: _____ ☐ AM ☐ PM

Temp: _____

Rotating Perishable Products Using FIFO

The use of the FIFO system is usually up to the manager, sous chef, or executive chef, or a steward, if available. The FIFO system is a simple but effective way to ensure that older product is used before newer product so that the first items placed in storage are the first to be taken out to be used. Food that is added should be placed behind the existing product. In FIFO, the key is moving the older product in front of or on top of the newer product. Sometimes putting older product in a separate container makes it an easier reach for the employees. Keeping the newer product in its original box in hard-to-reach places is the safest way to work within this type of system.

A cooler should be monitored on a daily basis to ensure that no products are left behind or get lost on a lonely shelf. This is particularly important with produce and perishable items with a very short shelf life.

Products should have labels that can be marked with the date on which the product was stored. They are called "use first" labels.

Inventory Products Regularly

Each establishment should have inventory schedules for the freezer, cooler, and dry goods sections of its storage. Whatever the schedule in your enterprise, you should follow it regularly.

Taking monthly inventory prevents waste and avoids the unpleasant surprise of unused products. This is part of an organized, monitored, orderly, storage system and should not be a major project if your entire product line has a designated position in storage.

Use a list of all the items that you regularly stock. Write the number on hand and compare it to the number recommended for each item. Use your results to adjust ordering in the future.

Maintaining Perpetual Inventory

Perpetual inventory can help maintain better control over your inventory. **Perpetual inventory** is a system of records used to track all goods entering and leaving a storeroom. It allows you to see the inventory on hand at any given point in time, usually daily or weekly. During the week, management must record all requisitions, purchases, sales and manager comps (menu items given to customers for free), and wasted product on one sheet. (See *Exhibit 3h*.)

The beginning inventory each day is the ending inventory of the previous day. Calculate the ending inventory this way:

Total on hand − Total used = Ending inventory

Here is another way to calculate ending inventory:

$$\left(\begin{array}{c} \textbf{Beginning} \\ \textbf{inventory} \end{array} + \textbf{Purchased} \right) - \left(\textbf{Sold} + \textbf{Comped} \right) = \begin{array}{c} \textbf{Ending} \\ \textbf{inventory} \end{array}$$

Using the figures from Monday in *Exhibit 3h*, ending inventory is calculated as follows:

$$\left(14 + 45 \right) - \left(34 + 6 \right) = 19$$

Exhibit 3h

Perpetual Calculations

Steaks	Total on Hand		Total Used		
	Beginning Inventory	Purchased	Sold	Comped	Ending Inventory
Monday	14	45	34	6	19
Tuesday	19	45	40	2	22
Wednesday	22	90	74	4	34
Thursday		90	69	5	
Friday		110	85	3	
Saturday		115	93	2	
Sunday		45	36	5	

Activity

Perpetual Inventory

Use the ending inventory from Wednesday to calculate the beginning inventory and ending inventory for the remaining days of the week.

Steaks	Total on Hand		Total Used		
	Beginning Inventory	Purchased	Sold	Comped	Ending Inventory
Monday	14	45	34	6	19
Tuesday	19	45	40	2	22
Wednesday	22	90	74	4	34
Thursday		90	69	5	
Friday		110	85	3	
Saturday		115	93	2	
Sunday		45	36	5	

Obtaining the Maximum Shelf Life of Perishable Goods

Food technologists and chemists have identified two principle factors that explain why perishable food spoils:

■ The chemical effect of air—**oxidation,** which is the combination of a substance with oxygen

■ Growth of aerobic microorganisms (for example, bacteria in need of air to survive)

Both of those factors, either alone or together, will bring changes in odor, flavor, color, and texture and have the same end effect: deterioration in quality. Proper refrigeration can slow this process but will not stop it. Through research, however, the shelf life of perishable food such as meat, poultry, fish, and produce has dramatically increased.

Fish

Following are several considerations for storing fish, both frozen and flash-frozen.

Flash Freezing

Flash freezing means that the food has been frozen solid in a short period of time. Most flash-freezing plants hold their product at a constant −10°F (−23°C) and pack it in dry ice before it gets shipped to restaurants.

Fish can be freshly caught, processed (descaled, drained, or pan dressed and even filleted) and frozen solid in a matter of hours. Flash-frozen fish has a better look and feel without using any preservatives. It is not subject to freezer burn. Texture and flavor do not change through defrosting the product.

Some fishing ships have flash-freezing capability onboard. The overall quality of the seafood will not be higher after flash freezing, but it will maintain the quality with which the seafood was caught. Flash freezing is also possible with other products such as meat.

Important Quality Issues with Frozen Fish

Following are other important considerations concerning the quality of frozen fish:

■ Fish must be frozen airtight and as dry as possible.

■ Keep frozen fish at temperatures that will keep it frozen.

■ Label fish properly.

Think About It...

What can you do to prevent exposed steak bones from poking holes in the plastic sealing bag when you vacuum-pack individual portions?

■ Do not hold frozen fish longer than six months.

■ Defrost in refrigerator in twenty-four hours or under running cold water in one hour.

■ Do not refreeze fish.

Quality Issues with Other Fish Products

Whole fish must be used immediately. If not cooked, it must be cleaned completely (drained) to avoid belly burn. Belly burn is the deterioration of the toxins in the intestines that spoils the meat of the fish. If fish is drained, pan dressed, and/or cut into fillets, storage issues are the same as above.

Poultry

To store fresh poultry without jeopardizing any food quality, you should keep it on ice as cold as possible, and always on the lowest shelf in the cooler or refrigerator. This keeps the food in a safe environment and reduces the chance of cross-contamination.

Fresh and Prepared Meat

Raw meat, especially portion-cut steak, should be kept in vacuum-sealed pouches in the box in which they arrived. This will avoid the mix-up of product during requisitioning by the cooks when they pull product for their prep list.

Fresh meat and game products should be stored away from ready-to-eat food, even if vacuum sealed. The packaging should be kept closed to ensure the proper wet aging. If you receive fresh meat, especially game (e.g., leg of lamb, hotel rack of lamb, etc.) in butcher paper, you must wrap it in airtight, moisture-proof material to prevent blood leakage and the drying out of the product.

For sausage and similar product, follow the expiration date on the packaging and keep the product as cool as possible. Wrap leftovers tightly or vacuum-pack them in a new bag to seal and shut out oxidation.

Smoked or cured products should be handled like any other product. Most of the time, the chef hangs smoked or cured product in the cooler. This saves some room on the shelves and allows the cool air to circulate freely around the product.

Exhibit 3i

Storage of Dairy Products

Product	Temperature	Time
Milk	In cooler at 41°F (5°C) or lower	Maximum of fourteen days. However, discard after use-by or expiration date.
Ultra-pasteurized milk	Unopened—no need to refrigerate	
	Opened—In cooler at 41°F (5°C) or lower	Maximum of fourteen days
Frozen milk products, such as ice cream	In freezer at temperature to keep frozen	Two to four months

Exhibit 3j

Storage of Cheese

Category	Product	Days (unopened)	Days (opened)
Soft unripened cheese	Cottage	Ten to thirty days	Two weeks
	Ricotta	Five days	Five days maximum
Ripened or cured cheese	Cheddar, Edam, Gouda, Swiss, Brick, etc.	Three to six months	Three to four weeks; sliced, two weeks

Dairy Products

The USDA-recommended storage times for dairy products as shown in *Exhibit 3i*.

Cheese Products

There are two potential quality problems with cheese: drying out and developing mold. Mold that indicates spoilage grows from the inside of some cheese. If mold appears on the outside, the cheese should be discarded.

The best way to take care of cheese is to keep it in the original wrapper or covering. If that is not possible, rub some oil on the cheese and wrap it tightly in clinging plastic wrap to keep all air and moisture away from the surface. The storage times shown in *Exhibit 3j* are guidelines for maintaining the quality of cheese in refrigeration after purchase.

Fruit and Vegetables

There are two considerations for storing fruit and vegetables: ethylene gas exchange and variations in temperature in the cooler.

Vendors, as a quality standard, have a controlled atmosphere in their warehouses. In sealed warehouses, the vendor can precisely control the temperature, humidity, and composition of gases in the atmosphere. Produce may be stored months longer than usual, staying at its best. Food vendors usually minimize the amount of oxygen and increase the concentration of carbon dioxide in the storeroom to reduce spoilage, enhance shelf life, and preserve the quality of the product.

Ethylene Gas Exchange

Consider the gas exchange of some fruit and vegetables when you decide where to store them. Some fruit and vegetables produce a colorless gas called **ethylene gas** that increases the ripening process. Unfortunately, this gas may accelerate deterioration of products nearby.

Knowing that ethylene gas is helping to increase the ripening process makes it possible to have a separate ripening room for produce. This process of controlled and uniform ripening enhances food quality immensely. *Exhibit 3k* shows a table of items that create ethylene gas and some items damaged by it.

Exhibit 3k

Ethylene Gas Interactions

Generate Ethylene Gas	Can Be Spoiled by Ethylene Gas
Apples	Asparagus
Apricots	Belgian endive
Avocados	Broccoli
Bananas, ripening	Cabbage
Cantaloupe	Carrots
Citrus fruit, except grapefruit	Cucumbers
Figs	Cut flowers (edible or for decoration)
Grapes	Eggplant
Honeydew	Green beans
Kiwifruit, ripe	Kale
Mangos	Leafy greens
Mushrooms	Parsley
Nectarines	Peas
Peaches	Peppers
Pears	Potatoes
Tomatoes	Spinach
Watermelon	Summer squash

Placing Produce Correctly in the Cooler

Green vegetables must be placed carefully in a cooler. A cooler has cold and warm spots, and vegetables can be sensitive to temperature variations of a few degrees. Therefore, it is imperative to know the temperatures in your cooler and to know which vegetables are more sensitive than others.

For example, here is a foodservice manager describing a situation he encountered with vegetables spoiling:

"Green vegetables were my worst nightmare. Starting with asparagus to fresh spinach, those items spoiled quickly in my restaurant's coolers. The day I finally spoke with my food vendor about it was very fortunate. He was able to save the restaurant some money when he told me where to place the vegetables inside the cooler.

I rearranged my cooler, and two weeks later I had prolonged the shelf life of my leafy greens tremendously. I was very thankful to my vendor, although he lost the revenue of an extra case of spinach every month."

See *Exhibit 3l* for a guide to placing produce correctly in the cooler.

Exhibit 3l

Layout of Fruit and Vegetables in a Cooler

33–35°F (.6-1.7°C)	
Artichokes	Leaf lettuce
Broccoli	Peaches
Carrots	Radishes
Cauliflower	Celery
Cherries	Grapes

35–39°F (1.7-3.9°C)	
Squash	Zucchini
Sprouts	Green onions

40–45°F (4-7°C)	
Bell peppers	Pineapple
Green beans	Cucumbers

50-65°F (10-18.3°C)	
Potatoes	Tomatoes
Bananas	Onions

Blower

33–35°F

Cooler

35–39°F   35–39°F

35–39°F   35–39°F

50–65°F (outside)   50–65°F (outside)

33–35°F (.6-1.7°C)	
Apples	Lettuce
Apricots	Mushrooms
Asparagus	Strawberries
Blueberries	Kiwifruit
Cabbage	Corn

35–39°F (1.7-3.9°C)	
Herbs	Pears
Parsley	Cantaloupe

40–45°F (4-7°C)	
Lemons/limes	Grapefruit
Eggplant	Avocado

50-65°F (10-18.3°C)	
Sweet potatoes	Squash (hard shell)

Activity

Produce Storage Items

Talk with a produce person at a local produce store about which fruit and vegetables should be stored separately or next to each other. Ask the produce manager about the following combinations and discuss in class what can happen with the produce.

■ Bananas next to tomatoes ■ Onions next to avocados

Discuss in class the different combinations that worked well and how the produce manager separated the items.

Think About It...

What fruit can be used to preserve green leaf vegetables in the cooler?

Herbs

In general, herbs should be stored in airtight containers, with as little light as possible. Plastic foam boxes help to ensure the longest possible shelf life of herbs. You can store them in an airtight container or bag up to five days in a refrigerator.

If you want to store herbs up to ten days (depending on the herb), put the herb stem down in a water container where the ends are covered up to one inch. Put an airtight cover on it and change the water every two days. Before you use any herbs, wash them and blot them dry with paper towels.

Make sure whatever container you choose, according to the amount of herbs you have, is not stored on a cold spot in your cooler. If your herbs start freezing, they will turn brown and will lose all of their important fragrance, texture, and flavor.

Equipment to Preserve Food Products

Currently, equipment is being developed that plays a role in quality assurance and extending the shelf life of some products. This equipment maintains food temperature and cools or heats food more quickly than earlier storage setups. Examples include:

■ **Salad crispers**—Large, stainless steel containers that can hold large amounts of salad ingredients, as well as cold cuts. Ethylene gas is removed from the environment.

■ **Computer-controlled quick chillers**—Large equipment cools warm food quickly. Computer controls keep track of temperatures.

■ **Vacuum-packaging systems**—Single machine used to seal food, greatly extending the shelf life. Food is placed in a very thick plastic bag and then placed in the machine. Air is withdrawn, and the package is heat-sealed. Optionally, gases can be injected that preserve food longer.

Activity

Receiving an Invoice

Using this invoice, write on a separate sheet of paper what you would store first and where. This exercise should show how important it is to think quickly; otherwise you will lose product quickly.

MIDWEST FARMS, INC.
1134 County Line Road, Normal, Illinois 61761
PHONE 309 555 6794   FAX 309 555 6688

INVOICE No. _____ C1049-5 _____
DATE _____ 11/07/07 _____

CUSTOMER _____ The Breakfast Nook _____

QUANTITY	DESCRIPTION	WEIGHT	PRICE	TOTAL	QUANTITY	DESCRIPTION	WEIGHT	PRICE	TOTAL
5 lb	Ginger root	5#	2.22	11.11	1 case	Olive oil	25#	30.00	30.00
2 lb	Lemongrass	2#	1.39	2.78	1 case	Bacon, 15#	15#	1.83	27.50
2 lb	Mint, fresh	2#	8.33	16.67	2 case	Asparagus, 11# case	22#	25.56	51.11
2 lb	Oregano, fresh	2#	8.33	16.67	1 bag	Bean sprouts 10#	10#	5.56	5.56
4 bag	Shallots, dry 10#	40#	17.83	71.32	1 case	Beans, green	5#	31.11	31.11
1 gal	2% Milk	1#	2.50	2.50	5 lb	Beets, red	5#	6.00	6.00
1 tub	Sour cream, 5#	5#	5.50	2.50	1 case	Broccoli, 14 ct.	5#	21.11	21.11

SUBTOTAL $ 594.00

Past due invoices are subject to a 10% charge. Buyer agrees to pay collection and attorney's fees if legal action for collection is necessary. A $35.00 charge will be made for each NSF check.

Signature: _____

Signature indicates that the above has been satisfactorily received.

Canned and Specialty Goods

Canned goods have the longest shelf life of any product in the storeroom. If processed correctly, canned goods can remain safe until the seal is broken. For best quality (though not addressing safety), use canned goods within five years.

Manufacturers use codes to tell when a can was packed and, therefore, when it expires. The code tells when the food was produced. The codes vary by producer, but your supplier should be able to explain those to you. The Internet is also a good source of this information. Canned goods also contain preservatives to maintain quality. The preservatives that were used must be on the labels.

Sous vide, which is the cooking of various ingredients in a plastic pouch, and other specially packaged food items are shelf stable. Be sure to check and follow manufacturers' expiration dates.

Sugar, Flour, Rice

Considerations for storing these types of products include:

- Be sure they are stored in airtight containers.

- Be sure they are at least six inches off the floor.

- Label properly; many white and off-white products are easily confused if they are not labeled correctly.

Activity

Storage of Ingredients for Standardized Recipes

On the lines below, write the storage requirements for the ingredients of these standardized recipes. Write the storage area in which the ingredients must be stored. Write any time limits that must be observed or if an ingredient must be discarded by a specific date. This may require you to do some research.

French Onion Soup Ingredients	Storage Area	Time Limit
Onions	Dry Storage	2 months
Gruyère		
Croutons		
Sherry		
Stock		
Clarified butter		
Fresh thyme		

Apple Pie Ingredients	Storage Area	Time Limit
Apples		
Flour		
Sugar		
Shortening		
Nutmeg		
Cinnamon		

Summary

Standards are important when receiving food deliveries and then storing the food. A restaurant or foodservice operation can lose a great deal of quality if it accepts lower quality food than ordered. Food can lose a lot of quality quickly if it is not stored properly, especially the expensive perishables, such as meat and produce.

When selecting vendors, it is critical to be sure that they follow your guidance for delivery times and any specifications you have about receiving products. Be sure that you can reject products and that the vendor has a policy that is easy to work with. Evaluate vendors regularly, at least once a year.

Be very clear about who can sign in products at delivery. If no one has responsibility for signing, food cannot be stored promptly. Food that is not stored quickly can be time-temperature abused, cause a safety hazard if employees trip or fall, and be costly if food must be discarded.

Storing is one of the most important skills a foodservice professional needs. A manager must direct staff to rotate food in the cooler properly, using the FIFO system. Produce must be stored in the cooler in a zone appropriate for the food. Fruit and vegetables are sensitive to variations in temperature. If placed in the wrong section, the food can be ruined. Fruit and vegetables are also sensitive to ethylene gas. Produce that produces ethylene should be separated from produce that absorbs it.

Storing food properly also requires a system of labeling. Staff must label food carefully and completely. "Use first" labels should be placed on food. Some labels require details about who produced the food, the occasion, and the time it was produced. Using the correct labels helps avoid serving the wrong food.

Regular inventory cycles save money as well as preserve food quality by having the freshest food available for use.

Review Your Learning

1 Who on the staff is able to sign for receipt of deliveries?

A. Foodservice manager

B. Sauté cook

C. Buser

D. Waitstaff

2 Which is *not* a procedure needed for receiving and storage?

A. Shelf life should be tracked for all food.

B. Person(s) with signature authority will take responsibility for storing food promptly.

C. Vendors need to be able to contact a person by name for a signature.

D. Staff needs to know responsibilities for receiving and storage.

3 Which is a safety requirement for the receiving area?

A. Nonskid floors

B. Hooks for hanging equipment

C. Icemaker

D. Cleaning equipment

4 Which case of chicken should be used first?

A. May 31, 2007

B. June 15, 2007

C. May 15, 2007

D. June 2, 2007

5 A great deal of food is lost due to

A. seasonal ordering.

B. improper storage.

C. careless receiving.

D. lack of vendor requirements.

6 Which is true of perpetual inventory?

A. Perpetual inventory requires careful record keeping.

B. Perpetual inventories are taken once per year.

C. Perpetual inventory involves counting items by hand.

D. Perpetual inventory includes physically weighing products.

7 Salad crispers, quick chillers, and vacuum packaging systems all contribute to

A. assuring food quality.

B. reducing food costs.

C. oxidizing food items.

D. reducing shelf life.

8 Which must be stored in refrigeration?

A. Potatoes

B. Onions

C. Berries

D. Garlic

Notes

Quality in Food Production

Inside This Chapter

- Preparation Methods to Enhance Food Quality
- Cooking Methods to Enhance Food Quality
- Maintaining Quality after the Cooking Phase

After completing this chapter, you should be able to:

- Describe processes that can add quality to food during the preparation stage.
- Describe ways to add quality to food during cooking.
- Explain how to select the correct method for cooking a particular meat.
- Describe classic sauces and other types of sauces.
- Explain how to select accompaniments and garnishes.
- Describe ways to maintain quality during holding, cooling, reheating, and serving.

Test Your Knowledge

1 **True or False:** Flavoring and seasoning refer to the same process. *(See p. 84.)*

2 **True or False:** Marinating is the process of soaking food in seasoned liquid. *(See p. 77.)*

3 **True or False:** Sautéing and pan-frying are the same process. *(See p. 82.)*

4 **True or False:** Convenience food can sometimes be vacuum-packed. *(See p. 91.)*

5 **True or False:** Checking plates immediately before serving is a good, inexpensive way to ensure quality. *(See p. 92.)*

Key Terms

PREPARING MEATS

Aging

Blade tenderizing

Brining

Connective tissue

Curing

Dry aging

Kosher salt

Mallet

Marinade

Marinating

Needle tenderizing

Pounding

Scoring

Smoking

Tenderizing

Vacuum packaging

Wet aging

COOKING

Baking

Blanching

Boiling

Braising

Broiling

Browned

Combination method

Deep-frying (basket, swimming)

Deglazing

Dry heat

Flavoring

Frying

Grilling

Herbs

Moist heat

Pan-frying

Poaching (shallow, submerged)

Roasting

Sautéing

Seared

Seasoning

Simmering

Spices

Steaming

Stewing

SAUCES

Arrowroot

Béchamel sauce

Beurre manié

Blond roux

Brown roux

Brown sauce

Classic sauce

Demi-glace

Espagnole sauce

Hollandaise sauce

Liaison

Mirepoix

Modern sauce

Mother sauce

Nappe

Roux

Slurry

Small sauce

Thickener

Tomato sauce

Velouté sauce

White roux

MISCELLANEOUS

Appearance

Aroma

Center of the plate

Convenience food

Garnish

Nonfunctional garnish (NFG)

Shelf-stable

Texture

Introduction

In your position as a restaurant or foodservice manager, you will learn about many product and quality issues. Your role, professional input, and working habits are key to ensuring that food and menu items are produced to standards that enhance quality.

The two key phases in the flow of food that determine a quality end product are preparation and cooking. Learning the basic principles of quality in food production is key to solving the mystery of quality and its associated problems. Knowing how to select cooking methods, add flavorings and seasonings, and choose sauces, accompaniments, and garnishes, will help bring out the quality of food.

Your knowledge of applying the correct methods to raw ingredients and skill at executing these methods will produce food of high quality that will continually appeal to customers. In this chapter, you will learn about these methods, as well as recent developments in packaging and new equipment that can reduce preparation and cooking time. You must also understand the role of convenience food, and how to hold, cool, and reheat food without loss of quality.

Preparation Methods to Enhance Food Quality

Preparing food properly ensures that the ingredients are in the correct form for cooking. Preparation methods can be applied to all the ingredients of a meal; in this section, methods to prepare vegetables and meat are described.

Preparing Vegetables

If a chef can cut vegetables quickly and produce a uniform product, this will ensure several quality factors in the cooking process. Consistently cut vegetables produce a uniform size and shape, which allow chefs to calculate the cooking time precisely. These cuts not only look appealing, but also are the basis of standardized recipes.

An important skill for chefs is to be able to perform the classic knife cuts quickly. It takes practice to learn and maintain these skills. *Exhibit 4a* on the next page outlines the various classic vegetable cuts. These cuts are part of the universal language of culinarians.

Exhibit 4a

Classic Uniform Vegetable Cuts

	Basic Shape	Name	Size
	**Round**	Rondelle: disk-shaped slices	Varies, but each piece should be the same size. Cut perpendicular to the food.
		Diagonal: oval-shaped slices	Varies, but each piece should be the same size. Cut at an angle to the food.
	**Stick**	Batonnet	2″ × ¼″ × ¼″
		Julienne	2″ × ⅛″ × ⅛″
	**Cube**	Large dice	¾″ × ¾″ × ¾″
		Medium dice	½″ × ½″ × ½″
		Small dice	¼″ × ¼″ × ¼″ (start with batonnet)
		Brunoise	⅛″ × ⅛″ × ⅛″ (start with julienne)
	**Round/Square**	Paysanne	Basic shape depends on type of vegetable. Pieces are uniformly ½″ × ½″ × ⅛″.
	**Thin Strip**	Chiffonade	Roll leafy greens or herbs into a tube, then cut into thin strips.

Some techniques will result in varying cuts, depending on the type of vegetable used.

Preparing Meat

There are several processes that can be applied to meats to enhance the flavor or make tougher grades of meat more tender. Most of the methods involve a chemical process or physical treatment of the meat to break down the **connective tissue,** which is the tough part of the meat. This process is referred to as **tenderizing.**

Tenderizing

Tenderizing refers to any method used to break down connective tissue in meat. Here are some tenderizing methods that do not require any liquid:

- **Scoring**—Scoring is used on thin cuts of meat, such as veal and flank steak. Small cuts are made across the surface of the meat.

- **Pounding**—Special hammers, or **mallets,** are used to pound cuts of meat such as veal cutlets and chicken breasts.

- **Blade** or **needle tenderizing**—As meat is passed through a conveyer, a machine with multiple blades or needles penetrates the meat. The electric version of this machine looks similar to a pasta machine, and there are also hand-held varieties.

Marinating

Marinating is the process of soaking food in a liquid seasoned with herbs and spices to flavor it. For some meats, marinating tenderizes the product as well. The liquid, or **marinade,** usually includes oil, an acidic liquid such as vinegar or lemon juice, and herbs and spices. It can also be used to cook meat or as part of a sauce. Almost all ethnic cuisines use marinating in various forms.

Marinating has different effects on different types of meat and is typically used with a dry heat method, such as grilling or broiling. The time required for marinating ranges from one to several hours.

Marinating may also be accomplished by using a vacuum-sealed package, which results in a less time-consuming process. A vacuum-sealed package will cut the marinating time by about half, and will help to tenderize the meat as well.

Exhibit 4b

Aging Beef

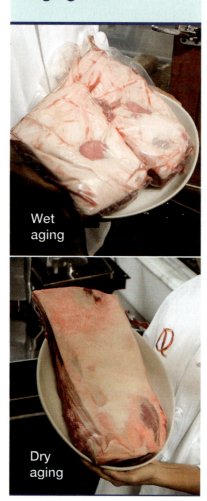

Wet aging

Dry aging

Aging

Aging is a process that tenderizes meat and is usually applied only to beef. Since aging beef requires time and storage space, it is generally more expensive than using fresh beef. There are two types of aging: wet aging and dry aging.

- **Wet aging** is sometimes referred to as **vacuum packaging.** Small portions of beef are placed in a thick plastic bag, all the air is vacuumed out, and the bag is sealed. (See *Exhibit 4b.*) The beef is then refrigerated for up to six weeks. During this time, the enzymes in the blood and flesh start breaking down the tough fibers of the muscles. When the bag is opened, the beef may have an unpleasant odor, which is normal. The odor will dissipate quickly after the beef is rinsed under cold water. There is usually no loss of yield in this aging process.

- **Dry aging** requires careful handling in special coolers and is usually done by specialty vendors using large cuts of beef. Air circulates at precise temperatures around the beef for a period of time determined by its size, temperature requirements, and other criteria. (See *Exhibit 4b.*) In addition to the costs of storage and handling, the meat can shrink up to 20 percent. Because of these costs and shrinkage, dry-aged beef is usually served in upscale restaurants or prime steakhouses.

Curing, Smoking, and Brining

Curing and smoking are methods that have been used for centuries to process meats.

Curing adds flavor in addition to preserving the meat. The most common curing method is to use salt and a combination of sodium nitrites and sodium nitrates. (See *Exhibit 4c.*) Sugars, herbs, spices, and flavored alcohol can be added for additional flavor.

Covering meat with salt breaks down its connective tissue. The length of time for this process depends on the size of the cut of meat. For example, the time for curing some pork products is one to one-and-a-half days per pound.

Sodium nitrite ($NaNO_2$), a salt used for curing meat, prevents bacteria that causes botulism from forming in meats. By the time the meat is cured, the chemical has dissipated. Sodium nitrite is colored pink to distinguish it from table salt. It gives meat its characteristic pink color. Sodium nitrate ($NaNO_3$) is also sometimes used in curing, but it should generally be avoided. It lasts longer in meats than nitrites, and can break down when heated to high temperatures.

Exhibit 4c

Processing Meats

Curing

Smoking

Brining

Smoking is used to add a special, characteristic smell of the material used to create the smoke. Smoking requires a special container, a source of smoke and heat, and a way for the smoke to be exhausted. (See *Exhibit 4c.*) For safety reasons, only meat, poultry, and fish that have been previously cured should be smoked, but this does not apply to cheese. Food can be either cold smoked or hot smoked. During cold smoking, food spends a period of time between 35°F (2°C) and 140°F (60°C).

Brining is a method of tenderizing and plumping lean meat, poultry, and pork. The meat is soaked in a solution of salted water, usually with sugar added, and sometimes spices. The proportion of salt is about 20 percent, or one-quarter to one-half cup of Kosher salt to one quart of water. (See *Exhibit 4c.*) **Kosher salt** is preferred because its texture is coarser and flakier than regular table salt. Sugar is often added—two tablespoons to one-half cup for one quart of water.

The meat is placed in a plastic bag with the brine mixture, and then sealed and refrigerated for one hour per pound. During cooking, the meat will remain plump because of the brine, and the sugar will soften the taste of the salt. If thicker cuts are used, such as ham or corned beef, the brine may be injected into the meat itself. Hams that have been brined may then be smoked.

Cooking Methods to Enhance Food Quality

Cooking is the major process used to transform various ingredients into a meal that is memorable to customers. Advances in technology have provided many options in the cooking phase. In this section, you will learn about methods used to transform food from its raw or preparation stage to an item that is served to customers. The key is to know products well enough to choose the correct cooking method and accompaniments.

Choosing the Correct Cooking Method

Selecting the correct cooking method to match a type of meat or other ingredient depends on knowing your product. You will need to choose among a variety of cooking methods that produce different results.

Considerations in the Kitchen

When selecting a cooking method, the primary task is to match a method to a type of food or cut of meat. When planning menus, you must keep in mind other factors, such as the cooking time.

New technology offers the possibility of cutting the cooking time for braising, roasting, or overnight cooking in half, but some cooking methods take a longer time even in the special cooking equipment that is now available.

Also consider the "footprint," or amount of oven and stove space required for each method so production in the kitchen runs smoothly. If the majority of items in an establishment require broiling, for example, the kitchen must be planned to have an increased amount of broiling equipment.

Three Basic Cooking Methods

There are three basic methods for cooking: moist heat, dry heat, and a combination of the two. The objective of any cooking method is to yield a tender product. If certain types of meat, poultry, fish, or vegetables are cooked too long, they will become tough or lose nutrients, a good appearance, and quality. Knowing the product itself, the temperature to be applied, and the length of cooking time are factors that affect the selection of a cooking method. Examples of the three basic methods are listed in *Exhibit 4d*.

Method 1: Moist Heat

Food is cooked submerged in liquid, or just above the liquid. The liquid may be water or stock. Depending on the temperature of the liquid and the length of time, moist heat makes certain products tender.

- **Boiling**—Liquid is maintained at the boiling point, 212°F (100°C), and food is submerged the entire time. Pasta needs to be boiled to make it edible and to bring out its texture.

- **Simmering**—Liquid is maintained at a hot temperature, but not boiling, and usually bubbles slightly. This method helps tenderize certain vegetables and tough meats.

- **Poaching**—There are two variations of poaching: **shallow poaching** and **submerged poaching.** The temperature of the liquid is the same in both, but the food is completely covered with liquid in submerged poaching. In shallow poaching, the food is placed on vegetables and half-covered with liquid. Usually a light cover, such as buttered parchment paper with a hole in the middle, is used as a lid to finish the cooking. The parchment lets out the steam and protects the food from becoming dry.

- **Steaming**—Food is cooked above a hot liquid, but the liquid never actually touches the food. This method is less likely to be used when cooking protein, but it is useful when cooking vegetables, since nutrients are not washed away. New equipment is available that specializes in steam and combination cooking.

■ **Blanching**—Food is cooked very briefly in hot water, and then cooled very quickly; the food may not be cooked all the way through. This process brings out the color in vegetables and kills the enzymes. Blanching is useful to cut cooking time during last-minute preparations.

Method 2: Dry Heat

Heat is applied without any water; fat may be used.

■ **Broiling**—High heat is applied from above, usually to tender cuts of meat and some vegetables. Meat gets quickly browned on the outside, while the inside stays tender.

■ **Grilling**—Heat is applied from below, rather than above; the principles are similar to broiling. Grilling is not the preferred method for small individual food items because the food could fall through the grill and burn.

Exhibit 4d

Cooking Methods

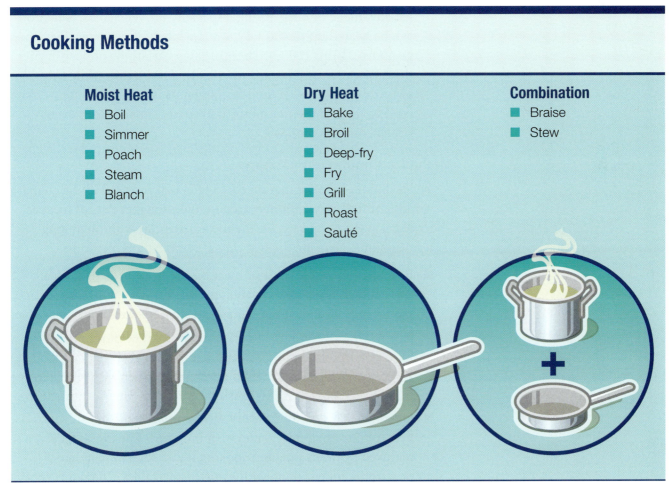

Moist Heat	Dry Heat	Combination
■ Boil	■ Bake	■ Braise
■ Simmer	■ Broil	■ Stew
■ Poach	■ Deep-fry	
■ Steam	■ Fry	
■ Blanch	■ Grill	
	■ Roast	
	■ Sauté	

Think About It...

Why isn't cooking in oil or fat considered moist heat?

Oil and fat have different properties than water, affect food differently, and can be heated up to 400°F (204°C). Vegetable oils can be heated to a higher temperature than animal fats before they will burn.

■ **Baking** and **roasting**—Food is cooked in an open dish or on a rack in an oven. Baking usually refers to breads and pastries, while roasting refers to meats. As the meat roasts, the juices from the meat drip into the bottom of a drip pan. The juices can then be used for a sauce or gravy.

■ **Sautéing**—Meat, usually thinly cut, is quickly cooked with a small amount of fat in a very hot pan on the stovetop. The juices that remain in the pan after cooking can be used for a sauce or gravy. When liquids, such as wine, water, or lemon juice, are added to the residue in the pan to make a sauce, it is called **deglazing.**

■ **Frying** or **pan-frying**—Meat, usually thinly cut as in sautéing, is quickly cooked—also using a moderate amount of fat in a very hot pan on the stovetop. In this method, meats are frequently breaded for more flavor and to seal in the meat's juices. There are not usually enough juices left in the pan to make a gravy or sauce.

■ **Deep-frying**—Food is submerged in hot oil for a short amount of time, until it turns brown. Deep-frying does not tenderize most meats and is not often used on beef, veal, lamb, or pork. An advantage of deep-frying, especially for vegetables, is that oil can be heated up to 400°F (204°C), while boiling water does not go above 212°F (100°C). There are two variations of deep-frying: the **basket method** is used for smaller food items, while the **swimming method** is used for larger, usually battered items that need to float in the hot oil until properly cooked to an even, golden-brown color.

Method 3: Combination Method

The technique of combination cooking is well accepted in the culinary world. This technique is often used to make tougher cuts of meat as tender as possible and to give the meat better flavor through long-term cooking. Here are the two classic combination methods:

■ **Braising**—A whole roast of meat is **seared,** or **browned,** on all sides at high heat, creating an appealing brown color. After searing, the meat is covered about halfway in a liquid (sometimes red wine) and slowly cooked with root vegetables. The liquid produces an excellent base for a sauce. Large cuts of meat are usually braised whole and then cut into serving-size portions in the restaurant's kitchen or by a carver at a guest's table.

■ **Stewing**—This method is very similar to braising, but the meat is first cut into small pieces and then browned. The excess fat is removed from the pot, and cooking liquid such as wine, stock, or water is added, along with assorted vegetables. The pot is kept covered, and the liquid should not boil.

Exhibit 4e summarizes the different cooking methods and shows types of food that are well suited to each method. The exhibit also outlines types of food that can lose quality if cooked using a particular method.

Exhibit 4e

Advantages/Disadvantages of Cooking Methods for Different Food

Cooking Method	Good for	Bad for
Moist Heat	*Overall, results in a more delicate product, except for the blanching method.*	
Boil	Dense, tough products such as shoulder cuts of meat, and hardy root vegetables	Already tender products, such as fish and asparagus, or products with a high water content
Simmer	Fish and delicate vegetables or fruit	Dense, tough meat products
Poach	Fish, poultry, and delicate vegetables	Dense, tough meat products
Steam	Fish and vegetables, especially greens	Dense, tough meat products
Blanch	Vegetables, especially greens	Dense, tough meat products
Dry Heat	*Overall, results in more tender protein and more sturdy produce.*	
Bake/roast	Products with a high water content, whole fish, and seafood	Tough cuts of meat or leafy green vegetables
Broil	Meat products, fish, sturdy vegetables, and certain fruit	Soft or too-small products
Deep-fry/fry	Products with high starch content and low water content	Tough cuts of meat or leafy green vegetables
Grill	Meat products, fish, sturdy vegetables, and certain fruit	Soft or too-small products
Sauté	Universal, but for some products it may be necessary to finish the cooking process with a moist heat method	
Combination	*Overall, enhances very tough protein and high-fiber produce.*	
Braise	Tough cuts of meat and hardy root vegetables; can be used for large pieces of meat	Already tender products or products with high water content
Stew	Tough cuts of meat and hardy root vegetables; meat is usually cut into small pieces	Already tender products or products with high water content

Activity

Select the Correct Cooking Method

After reviewing the cooking methods and looking at the chart in *Exhibit 4e*, choose the correct cooking method and suggest the specific cooking technique to ensure the highest possible retention or enhancement of food quality in the described product. Once finished, discuss the possible answers, especially those in which there may be more than one correct method or technique.

Product	Cooking Method	Cooking Technique
New York strip steak		
Beef chuck		
Rack of lamb		
Spinach		
Collard greens		
Asparagus		
Tilapia (fish)		
Mussels		
Pasta		

Flavoring and Seasoning

It is common to confuse flavoring and seasoning. **Flavoring** brings out the natural flavor of a food by adding herbs and spices, while **seasoning** refers to adding salt and pepper. Both must be handled carefully, so that food is not overpowered by flavoring or seasoning.

Flavoring: Herbs and Spices

Each food, from seafood to meat, or fruit to nuts, has its own distinct flavor and aroma. The goal is to bring out this flavor. This is frequently done with herbs and spices, which can also add creativity to a menu item.

When selecting a flavoring, choose one that complements the main dish, not one that may be overpowering. It is important to develop a strong sense for the right or wrong flavor profile of a particular food in order to enhance a dish. It is also critical to know when to add the flavoring during the cooking process.

Herbs are the leaves from plants that have a characteristic flavor. Herbs should not cover up the flavor profile of the main item, but instead accompany the food's flavors. Herbs may be fresh or dried. It is up to the chef and manager to balance the cost and benefits of using fresh herbs, which are more expensive and more difficult to keep, or dried herbs, which last longer but may not produce the same effect. In most classical applications, herbs are introduced to a dish right before serving to ensure that the heat of the dish does not dissipate the herbs' delicate aroma and flavor.

Spices often come from the seeds of plants and are nearly always used in dried form. They have a stronger and more pungent flavor than herbs, but still have the purpose of supporting a dish. If spices are used too heavily, they can easily spoil any dish; a pinch too much can make a dish completely inedible and ruin the spice's intended purpose.

Seasoning: Salt and Pepper

Seasoning refers to adding salt and pepper. Salt and pepper should be used only according to standardized recipes, since too much salt will overpower an entire dish. It is best to let the customer do any final seasoning, since some customers may be on sodium-restricted diets. Most restaurants have salt and pepper shakers on guest tables.

Use salt and pepper at the beginning of the cooking process. This will ensure that sauces, butter, or other liquids will not wash off the seasoning. It will also ensure that if you use the sauté technique for a dish and deglaze the pan with a liquid, the salt used will be incorporated into the sauce without having to add more.

Sauces

Sauces complement a dish. When chosen and executed well, a sauce brings out the best qualities of the item it accompanies. Five sauces are considered the basics of classic French cuisine, and they require skill and practice to prepare. There are also newer sauces that are not as rich as classic sauces and represent other cuisines. Some of them are easier and less costly to prepare.

Sauces are liquid-based, generally have a thickener, and add additional quality factors to a dish. Texture, appearance, flavor, and nutritional value are the keys to a quality sauce. This section describes thickening agents, classic sauces, and modern sauces.

Thickening Agents

A **thickener** is any ingredient that is added to a liquid to make it thicker. An important skill is to know which thickener works best with which flavoring and sauce. There are many types of thickeners.

A **roux** is a mixture of equal parts flour and butter, which is cooked on the stove at a low temperature and used as the basis of various sauces. If it is cooked for a short time, it is called a **white roux.** If it is cooked longer and starts to develop a light brown color, it is called a **blond roux.** If the basic roux is cooked until it becomes brown, it is called a **brown roux.** Note the differences in the colors of the three types of roux in *Exhibit 4f.* An uncooked roux is called a **beurre manié** and follows the same thickening principle.

Another thickening agent is **slurry,** a combination of cold liquid and cornstarch, which is mixed and then brought to a simmer. When using a slurry, proper cooking time is needed to avoid having a starchy flavor in a sauce.

Exhibit 4f

Examples of Roux

Blonde roux

White roux

Brown roux

Some sauces are finished by a **liaison,** which is a thickening agent made of heavy cream and egg yolk. The thickener is tempered—hot liquid is slowly added to it to raise the temperature without curdling—and then mixed into the sauce. A reheating of this type of sauce is not recommended because the protein of the egg yolk will curdle the sauce.

Modern sauces have **arrowroot** as a thickening agent. Arrowroot—a starch that is obtained from the stem of a tropical American perennial herb—is used in many ethnic cuisines and is the only thickening agent that can be frozen and defrosted without losing its texture.

Classic or Mother Sauces

The **classic sauces** are also sometimes called **mother sauces,** since other sauces may be developed from them. These sauces take a considerable amount of time and practice to perfect. If you use one of the mother sauces for a derivative sauce (also known as a small sauce), prepare the mother sauce to a **nappe** consistency, which means to cover the back of a spoon.

There are five classic sauces in French cuisine (see *Exhibit 4g*):

- **Béchamel sauce** uses a large amount of flour, butter, and milk.

- **Velouté sauce** has been reinvented with the use of rice as a thickener, instead of flour and butter, and can also be used as a base for cream soups and vegetarian sauces.

- **Espagnole** or **brown sauce** is also incorrectly referred to as demi-glace. The difference is that **demi-glace** is half brown sauce and half brown stock, which is then reduced by half. Brown sauce is meat stock plus brown roux and mirepoix. **Mirepoix** is a combination of cooked vegetables, usually one-half onion, one-quarter celery, and one-quarter carrot, which is added to dishes to provide flavor.

- **Hollandaise sauce** consists of egg yolks beaten with a liquid such as lemon juice or vinegar. Whole butter or clarified warm butter is gradually beaten in until the consistency is a thick liquid. It should be served immediately.

- **Tomato sauce** uses fresh or canned tomatoes and may be thickened by simmering over low heat for a few hours.

Exhibit 4g

Classic Sauces

Classic Sauce	Thickener	Liquid
Béchamel sauce (white)	White roux	Milk
Velouté sauce (blond)	Blond roux	White stock (fish, veal, or chicken)
Espagnole sauce (brown)	Brown roux	Brown stock (beef or veal)
Hollandaise sauce (butter)	Egg yolks	Melted butter
Tomato sauce (red)	not applicable	Juice from tomatoes

Small and Modern Sauces

Other sauces can be made using ingredients and thickeners that are not as rich as the ones in classic sauces. Note that the "small sauces" are derived from the classic sauces.

Small sauces are made using any classic or mother sauce as the base and then adding different flavorings. These sauces are often named after the ingredients used. Examples include various cream sauces, horseradish, and châteaubriand.

Modern sauces, which are not based on rich ingredients such as butter and eggs, are becoming more popular. These sauces are based on vegetables and fruit, and their textures vary from smooth to chunky. Vegetable-based sauces may have additional seasonings added. *Exhibit 4h* lists basic information about these sauces.

Exhibit 4h

Other Types of Sauces

Sauce Type	Base	Additional Info
Chutney	Cooked relish that is made with chopped fruit or vegetables, herbs, and spices.	Texture is chunky; may be sweet, hot, or sweet and hot.
Salsa	Sauce made of chopped vegetables or fruit, chili peppers, and spices, either cooked or uncooked.	Often tomato based, sometimes spicy.
Coulis	Fruit or vegetables are puréed in a blender or food processor and then strained through a sieve.	Fruit coulis may be used for desserts.

Exhibit 4i shows suggestions of sauces to accompany main courses. Try to use a sauce that complements the flavor of the food. Keep in mind that the color of a sauce is also important in the overall appearance of a dish.

Exhibit 4i

Examples of Sauces for Main Courses

Main Course	Suggested Sauce
New York Strip Steak	Demi-glace
Penne Pasta	Tomato sauce
Grilled Chicken Breast	Herb supreme sauce (velouté)
Steamed Alaskan Salmon	Tarragon hollandaise
Broiled Peppercorn-Crusted Swordfish Steak	Lemon-lime chutney

Accompaniments and Garnishes

Creative accompaniments and garnishes that are made from quality ingredients often distinguish a restaurant. They do not need to be expensive, but they should be of the highest quality. Some restaurants use their own signature items as accompaniments, such as creamed spinach or crosscut, deep-fried potatoes. Whatever accompaniment is used, it must enhance the main dish.

Garnishes

Garnishes are usually prepared separately, and sometimes with different cooking techniques than those used for the ingredients in the **center of the plate,** which is the main entrée. The quality of the garnish must enhance the entire dish. A garnish gives the chef and management an opportunity to be creative, as long as it does not overwhelm the main dish. A well-planned and well-prepared garnish can pay for itself by making an establishment stand out from its competitors.

For example, grilled salmon with a wedge of fresh baby pineapple is more appealing than a fish dish with a few sprinkles of dried cilantro. The customers' perception of "really fresh food" and "this is different" can make up for any difference in cost.

An operation should avoid any **nonfunctional garnish (NFG),** which is neither edible nor useful. For example, do not place a sprig of thyme in a grilled portobello burger. Thyme is not considered an ingredient, and eating it can be a jolting experience.

Plan a garnish that will complement the main course. When deciding if a garnish fits or not, note that some elements in judging quality are as important as those of the main course, such as appearance and texture.

Appearance is one of the two most important properties a garnish must fulfill on a plate. A garnish should have great visual impact; its color, generally in contrast to the main item, is one of the keys to the appeal of a dish. To retain color, some garnish items need to be blanched first.

Some examples of garnishes are a small bundle of fresh herbs over a braised veal shank, a fresh fruit skewer with a tuna sandwich, or chopped tricolor peppers sprinkled on orange pepper soup.

Texture or consistency is another important factor of a garnish and should complement the main course. For example, mashed potatoes topped with crisp fried onions, or a vegetable pizza with crumbles of feta cheese, both have fitting garnishes.

The **aroma,** or scent, of a garnish should be refreshing but not too strong. A lemon tuile or sesame cracker would be an appropriate enhancement to a salad or seafood course. Roasted cumin can add a wonderful smell to an Indian dish. A lemon wedge that garnishes a fish dish provides color and a light scent as well.

Accompaniments

An accompaniment must meet the same quality standards as the food in general. It should complement the main dish, and its preparation should be planned so that all items reach the customer's table at the correct temperature. The combination of items on a menu can help make a restaurant successful. Do not be offended, however, if customers ask for substitutions. No matter how carefully an establishment plans its accompaniments, there will always be people who ask for substitutions.

As a general guideline, think of "3 × 3 + 3," which means:

- Three colors on a plate
- Three textures on a plate
- Three flavors on a plate
- Three temperatures on a plate (for desserts or appetizers only)

Exhibit 4j lists examples of well-planned accompaniments for the center of the plate.

Exhibit 4j

Main Courses with Well-Planned Accompaniments

Main Course	Colors	Textures	Flavors	Temperature
Steak, peas, baked potato	Brown, green, off-white	Meaty, smooth, creamy	Grilled, fresh, mealy	Hot
Veal stew, broccoli, mashed potatoes	Brown, green, white	Saucy, crunchy, creamy	Hearty, fresh, mealy	Hot
Tricolor ravioli, tomato sauce, Parmesan cheese	Green, red, white	Al dente, saucy, grainy	Pasta, tomatoes, cheese	Hot

Activity

Add Accompaniments and Garnishes for These Main Courses

In this table, there are main course items listed in the first column. For each of these items, add in the appropriate column the accompaniments and garnishes that are needed to complete the meal: Sauce, Starch, Vegetable, and Garnish. When you are finished, compare your answers with the other students' ideas.

Main Course Item	Sauce	Starch	Vegetable	Garnish
Sautéed Chicken Breast				
Poached Salmon Fillet				
Grilled Filet Mignon				
Bison Burger				
Fried Cod				

Convenience Food

When **convenience food** was first introduced over fifty years ago, its main purpose was to provide completely cooked, safe food. Although these food items were safe, they sometimes lacked quality. New convenience products are now available, however, that are hard to distinguish from freshly cooked items and include such products as delicate desserts and sauces. These types of food have a **shelf-stable** capability, which means they can be stored for a long period of time. They may be packaged by a variety of methods: vacuum-sealed, freeze-dried, frozen, or cooled.

Preparing and cooking meals using only raw or unprocessed ingredients is sometimes thought to be better than using convenience food. This is true only if the highest quality ingredients are used and a standardized recipe is executed quickly and not changed in any way. If inferior products are used, or a recipe is altered in any way, the meal will not be of the highest standardized quality.

Other advantages of convenience food include:

■ **Convenience food is also useful for items that are sold in small quantities or not used very often.** For example, the shelf-stable capability of these products can provide a kitchen with various quick sauces, which would normally take about forty-five minutes each to prepare. These sauces can be stored for days and be ready to use in only a few minutes.

Think About It...

The term "cooking from scratch" started in Europe in the nineteenth century and referred to a line scratched in the ground to start a footrace. A runner had no advantage over another runner when starting from the scratch line.

■ **Convenience products save time and money by not tying up equipment and labor.** For example, a convenience package of basmati rice can be prepared in just sixty seconds, while cooking it from raw ingredients would take forty-five minutes and the use of an oven burner for that length of time.

■ **The quality of convenience food has improved so greatly that it is often hard to distinguish it from food cooked "from scratch."** These products are created by top chefs with vast experience in restaurant or foodservice establishments or as food producers. As Research and Development (R&D) chefs, they are creating new methods of handling food. They have helped to preserve the quality of products that previously were thought to be so fragile, or hard to execute, that no one would consider using them in a restaurant. R&D chefs develop standardized products that would usually take vast amounts of time to prepare in a restaurant. Examples include: instant hollandaise sauce, soufflé mixes, ready-to-use pastry creams, and clarified butter.

Maintaining Quality after the Cooking Phase

While preparation and cooking are the most important phases for producing a quality menu item, what happens after a dish has been cooked can affect quality as well. During each shift in an operation, the manager must ensure that the food coming out of the kitchen meets the operation's quality standards. Checking plates and their presentation against menu descriptions is the easiest, quickest, and least expensive way to do this. It also motivates your employees to ensure that each dish they prepare is completed with the same level of quality with which it began.

Additionally, an operation should consider ways to ensure quality throughout the holding, cooling, and reheating phases of a food item. Heating lamps and microwave ovens are traditional and effective methods for preserving quality. You should also consider exploring new, enhanced types of equipment, such as blast chillers or multipurpose ovens, for helping to preserve food through the phases in the flow of food.

Summary

There are many ways to bring out the taste of top-quality food. There are also ways to enhance the natural flavors of food items that are not of the highest quality, especially meats. Preparation and cooking in the flow of food are the main phases in which to add quality. Your skills at understanding and mastering these methods are at the heart of creating a successful restaurant or foodservice establishment.

There are several processes that can be applied to meats during the preparation phase. Marinating and physical means are methods of tenderizing meats. Aging, curing, and smoking can also be applied to enhance flavor. Curing is a method of preserving meats, while smoking should only be applied to previously cured meats.

There are three basic methods of cooking: moist heat, dry heat, and a combination of the two. It is critical to match the correct cooking method with the type of food being prepared. Sauces, both classic and other types, are important complements to a dish—as are flavorings, seasonings, accompaniments, and garnishes. Some combination of these elements can add to the quality of a meal and make it complete.

Finally, you must maintain quality during other phases of the flow of food. Both traditional methods and technologically advanced equipment can be helpful.

Review Your Learning

1 If you want to tenderize a tough piece of meat, which technique should *not* be used?

A. Marinating

B. Scoring

C. Aging

D. Blanching

2 The best way to cook a green vegetable to enhance its color is by

A. grilling.

B. broiling.

C. blanching.

D. boiling.

3 Which is a combination cooking method?

A. Stew

B. Grill

C. Sauté

D. Steam

4 To enhance the natural flavors of a protein in a dish, it is best to

A. put a heavy mother sauce on it.

B. have a heavily smoked accompaniment with it.

C. slightly salt and pepper it.

D. grill it until overdone.

5 Which is *not* a mother sauce?

A. Brown sauce

B. Demi-glace

C. Béchamel

D. Espagnole

6 What is the guideline to follow if you are composing a hot food entrée plate?

A. Three colors, three textures, all one flavor

B. One color, four textures, no flavor

C. Three colors, three textures, three flavors

D. Three temperatures, one texture, many flavors

7 What does NFG stand for?

A. National Foundation for Garnishes

B. Not for Garnish

C. Nonfunctional Garnish

D. Need for Garnish

8 What would be the most successful garnish on a fresh green salad with a very light dressing?

A. Heavily spiced orange marmalade sauce underneath the salad

B. Sesame cracker cornucopia surrounding the salad, sprinkled with red pepper brunoise

C. Hollowed-out cherry tomato with hollandaise sauce

D. Raw zucchini half-scooped with the salad inside it

9 Which is *not* an advantage of convenience food?

A. It is more shelf-stable than fresh-made foods.

B. It is portion controlled.

C. It is made in-house.

D. It provides nutritional value similar to fresh food.

Banquet and Buffet Food Production

After completing this chapter, you should be able to:

- Compare and contrast planning and production processes for banquets, buffets, and full-service meals.

- Identify procedures that will ensure quality food production in a banquet setting.

- Describe techniques to use on a production line for quantity events.

- Critique menu items that are feasible for banquets and buffets on and off premises.

Test Your Knowledge

1 **True or False:** Cooking and preparation areas in the kitchen are planned for efficiency. *(See p. 99.)*

2 **True or False:** All dishes for guests are finished on the line. *(See p. 99.)*

3 **True or False:** There are several people directing kitchen "traffic" in a restaurant serving individual dinners. *(See p. 110.)*

4 **True or False:** Managers use the same planning tools for banquets as for individual serving restaurants. *(See p. 97.)*

5 **True or False:** A production sheet is similar to a prep sheet. *(See pp. 108–109.)*

Key Terms

À la carte restaurant	Catering	In-house event
Al dente	Chafing dish	Line
Bain-marie	Combination oven	Line cook
Banquet	Expediter	Partially boil
Banquet/Buffet event order (BEO)	Fire	Precooking
Blanch off	Full-service restaurant	Production sheet
Buffet	Function sheet	Salamander
Carving station	Garde manger cook	Steam off
	Grill mark	

Introduction

Basic food production techniques are the same whether for à la carte meals, banquets, or buffets. **Banquets** are ceremonial dinners honoring a particular guest or occasion. **Buffets** are meals at which guests serve themselves from various dishes displayed on a table or sideboard. (See *Exhibit 5a.*) The logistics of producing quality food in quantity, however, are challenging, and there are unique ways to handle all settings.

Standardized recipes are the basis of quantity production in all restaurant and foodservice establishments. Whether establishments serve customers as they arrive, such as **à la carte** or **full-service restaurants** with a separate price for each item on the menu, or whether they serve customers with on-premises or off-premises banquets and buffet services, certain things must be in place to produce food in quantity and maintain quality. This chapter explores the factors for successfully producing quality food in quantity.

Exhibit 5a

Banquet

Buffet

Food production techniques are the same for banquets or buffets.

The Main Event—
From Four to Four Hundred

The main event is… the main event, whether it is an intimate dinner for two, a family outing with children, a wedding, or a fundraising dinner. The first similarity is that the meal starts with the standardized menu. The next similarity is that the menu is planned to meet the size of the kitchen. It may be difficult for a small dinner-only restaurant to prepare a delicate dessert for four hundred people that would be a highlight of the meal. Therefore, menu adjustments would need to be made. Full-service and banquet-service meals are kitchen intensive, while buffet-service meals are less kitchen intensive.

The main difference between à la carte meals, banquets, and buffets is in the serving times. A banquet, which is a fixed meal at a set time for a predefined number of guests, must be served in fifteen to forty-five minutes, whether for forty or four hundred people. À la carte diners come in to eat at various times, generally during the hours of service. Buffet service must have fresh food available when the customer places the order. The differences in preparation and service are considerable.

The table shown in *Exhibit 5b* on the next page highlights the special requirements of banquets and buffets.

Exhibit 5b

Comparison of Banquet Service to Buffets

	Banquet	Buffet
Menu Planning	To ensure the best quality food production in both of these examples of mass food production, keep the segments—preparation, cooking, holding, reheating, and serving—in mind when you create the menu.	
Preparation	Items must be prepared in large quantities. Preparation of items is usually broken down into smaller procedures. For example, the salad prep cook only peels all the vegetables for the banquet, but the garde manger cook takes the carrots and cuts them. The banquet or buffet chef will finish the cooking at the time of the party. There is more holding of raw material than for à la carte menu preparation.	
Cooking	When cooking in batches, it is sometimes difficult to maintain high quality. Finished food is still plated.	Food is finished and served in platters or service containers. Replenish serving dishes at least every two hours. Appropriate finishing is important for keeping the food quality high. Garnishes must be ready when the food is at its peak of quality and ready to serve.
Holding	Regardless of your equipment, a plated banquet must be served within fifteen to forty-five minutes. After this time, sauces, protein, and accompaniments will turn in flavor, texture, and temperature. Holding banquet food for a late party is very difficult if it is already plated. If it is still in containers, it will be in better shape and easier to reheat or keep warm in appropriate units.	Buffet items are usually held in their service containers. If an outside catering job, the food might be held in an aluminum service container ready to be placed in a chafing dish. Buffet food must look good for at least forty-five minutes to two hours on a buffet line before it has to be exchanged. It is especially difficult to retain crispness and color in green vegetables.
Cooling	Cooling is not an issue in banquets. Whatever food touched guests' tables will be discarded and not served again; therefore, there is no need for appropriate cooling.	If there is a service container that has never left the controlled environment of your kitchen, cool the item immediately (best in a blast chiller), and cover, label, and use it for the next shift or the next day.
Reheating	Not an issue	Correctly labeled items must be reheated according to proper food safety guidelines.
Serving	Precision work in plating and serving. Must be completed within fifteen to forty-five minutes. With certain holding units, this can be managed—plate covers are a major help as well.	Over one- to six-hour time frame. Service is minimal at tables. Replace food in serving dishes every two hours at least. Food in chafing dishes has the tendency to dry out or get dark on the sides; vegetables usually turn soggy and overdone. A buffet must look just as appealing and fresh in the last thirty minutes of service as in the first five minutes.

Factors That Influence Quantity Events

Not every full-service restaurant or foodservice establishment is in a position to also offer banquet and buffet services. That is because these services require specific capabilities and equipment to be carried out effectively. Restaurant or foodservice organizations that also want to provide banquet and buffet services must closely examine the factors involved in serving quantity events in order to determine if the organization wishes to pursue these types of services. Some of these factors are discussed below.

Making the Most of the Kitchen

The most critical factor in determining an operation's ability to offer banquets and catered events is the capacity of the kitchen. Without sufficient kitchen capacity, even the simplest banquet menu will quickly overwhelm the kitchen. If a kitchen has sufficient capacity, it must be layed out effectively. The kitchen layout affects efficiency and has an impact on how well the kitchen functions during quantity food production.

The following areas must be considered when evaluating kitchen capacity and efficiency:

1. Storing area
2. Cooking area
3. Hot preparation area
4. Assembly and carving area
5. Cooling area
6. Holding area
7. Reheating area

Equipment Used in the Kitchen

The number of pieces of equipment and the type and size of the equipment will depend on the menu, the size of the establishment, and the type of service. For example, the part of the kitchen closest to the service window where all dishes are prepared and finalized is called the **line.** The line includes both hot and cold food preparation. The area for cold-food production is usually off to the side somewhat, to keep food cool, but is still considered part of the production line. In each area of the kitchen, you will find certain pieces of equipment. These areas and the equipment in each are listed below according to the flow of food:

- **Storing**—Cooler and freezer cabinets.

- **Cooking**—Gas ranges; convection, conventional, and combination ovens; char-grills. **Combination ovens** are special

---

ovens that can perform several cooking functions, such as conventional, convection, and microwave, in one oven.

- **Hot preparation**—Deep-fryers.

- **Assembly and carving**—Kitchens usually have a large preparation board where last-minute cuts and carvings can be completed.

- **Cooling**—Cooling drawers.

- **Holding**—A **bain-marie** is a hot-water holding unit in which you can place metal containers with sauces, accompaniments, and other food that have to be kept over 140°F (60°C) in a food-safe environment. **Chafing dishes,** which also hold hot foods, are metal dishes or pans mounted above heating devices that are used to cook food or keep it warm at the table.

- **Reheating**—The reheating line consists of various types of cooking equipment; for example, **salamanders,** which are small broilers, as well as microwave and combination ovens.

Make the Menu Match the Type of Event

Just as a menu is planned for an à la carte restaurant, menus are planned for banquets that are aligned with the capacity of the kitchen. Offer menus to match the size and type of events that are being planned. If customers request changes, be sure that the changes are still possible in your facility.

Exhibit 5c

Benefits of a Diverse Menu

A well-balanced menu helps prevent overburdening the various cooking positions.

Menus for À La Carte Restaurants

A well-written and diverse menu can avoid overwhelming certain cooking stations and the cooks working on the line; for example, the grill cook. (See *Exhibit 5c.*)

Providing menu items that are balanced among the cooking stations helps lower the stress level. The planning and organization of scheduling the right amount of product coming from all the possible stations (grill, fry, broil, etc.) can determine how well your establishment will handle large quantities of guests and still be able to produce the highest-quality product for every order.

For example, do not concentrate the menu on one cooking station, such as the grill or sauté station. If several specials involve using the sauté station and 60 percent of the customers in one time segment order those specials, there may be too many sauté orders to complete the meals quickly without losing quality.

If you develop or revise menu items, be sure to test them before serving them at a busy meal time. For example, some great-tasting dishes may not be successful if the line cooks cannot put the finishing touches on the plate in a timely manner, or if the garnish is too brittle. The practicality of a dish is important, so if you want to offer a very delicate dish with a difficult plate presentation, then calculate more time for its preparation. Let the service staff know about new dishes so they can be prepared for the item. Allow a trial-and-error period for new dishes before you place them on the menu permanently.

Menus for Special Events

A special event calls for special planning to ensure that it runs smoothly. In contrast to à la carte meals, each event has requirements that may differ from previous or upcoming events. Each special event is planned with the sponsor.

Establishments usually have a selection of banquet and buffet menus for special events. The executive chef plans these menus so that the highest-quality food can be prepared without taxing the capabilities of the kitchen.

Many menu items on a banquet menu have a sauce as part of its presentation. From a chef's standpoint, the sauce is the key item on the plate. A sauce's flavor, texture, nutritional value, and color add a quality focus to the menu item. From a monetary point of view, a sauce is an inexpensive item that can make a major impact on a dish.

Think About It...

What is container service?

Buffet service is also called "container service." This comes from the use of standardized hotel pans, also called service containers.

Event Logistics

For the various types of special events and special logistic considerations, the first factor to consider is where an event will occur: at the establishment or off-site. The second consideration is whether it will be a sit-down event or a buffet.

Location of Special Events

Catering a single event for a particular occasion is a big segment of the restaurant and foodservice industry. There are two types of events—in-house and off-site.

In-house events, sometimes called on-premises or on-site catering, are held at your establishment. Food is served in a special room or in a tent near the establishment. Functions can be small or large and range from simple boxed lunches to complex plated dishes. The key is planning so that the kitchen can produce food for the event while the establishment is serving other banquets and à la carte meals.

Off-site catering is even more difficult to manage than in-house events due to the increase in food safety risks and food-quality concerns. In most situations, food is prepared in-house and then transported to the off-site location. During transportation, and even at the location, time-temperature abuse can be a problem. You must ensure that the food is properly prepared and that it stays out of the temperature danger zone (41°F to 135°F [5°C to 57°C]). For this reason, off-site events can be difficult to execute while still producing and maintaining high-quality food.

For example, imagine the challenge of planning and executing a catered buffet for a five-day outdoor public golf event that serves three hundred people twice a day and includes a five-course buffet with a **carving station**—a serving station at which the chef carves individual portions from a roasted beef, ham, or turkey. *Exhibit 5d* provides an estimate of the equipment and staff required to execute such an event.

Similarly, the "tasting events" some cities have during the summer, such as the Taste of Chicago, at which many restaurants sell signature items in multiple booths, pose special logistical challenges. To ensure proper food quality and safety, city health departments check vendors for violations and ask vendors to fix problems or close their booth and pay a fine. Keep in mind that your establishment is not exempt from serving safe food even though it is not being served at your establishment. The same food safety practices and procedures apply whether catering events on-site or off-premises.

Exhibit 5d

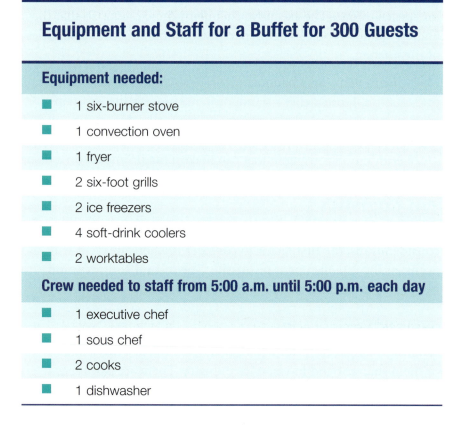

Equipment and Staff for a Buffet for 300 Guests

Equipment needed:

- 1 six-burner stove
- 1 convection oven
- 1 fryer
- 2 six-foot grills
- 2 ice freezers
- 4 soft-drink coolers
- 2 worktables

Crew needed to staff from 5:00 a.m. until 5:00 p.m. each day

- 1 executive chef
- 1 sous chef
- 2 cooks
- 1 dishwasher

Activity

Fundraiser

After a fundraiser for 350 people, the service manager gives the executive chef a note written by the fundraiser's event coordinator, who is also a regular guest at the "white-tablecloth" restaurant. It was the event coordinator's idea to have the fundraiser at this establishment to give the executive chef the opportunity to showcase his creativity. The event coordinator expected to be served his favorite menu item—filet mignon with béarnaise sauce, steamed asparagus, and potato au gratin.

On the day of the fundraiser, the executive chef was busy at the restaurant and away from the banquet kitchen. He put the sous chef in charge of the production and execution of the fundraising event. Five people, one of them new, prepped and plated the party. The new cook, who had recently graduated from a culinary program, had come highly recommended from the culinary school. During his trial time, he repeatedly had issues with following standardized recipes—not because of a lack of skill, but because he is very creative and already a good, self-confident cook.

In the note, the event coordinator briefly states that everything was great and better than expected, but he wanted to let the chef know how disappointed he was about the béarnaise sauce on the popular steak. It was not what he had previously experienced in the restaurant and he was wondering whether the chef had used a convenience (boxed) product instead of making it from scratch, or if there was another plausible explanation. He wants the executive chef to call him to discuss the situation.

You, the manager, instantly remember that you put the newly hired cook in charge of executing the standardized recipe for the béarnaise sauce—but you also admitted to the executive chef that you did not taste the finished product before plating. The sous chef now remembers mentioning to the new cook that the sauce looked too thin during plating, but it was too late at that point, and he decided not to change the sauce.

1 What do you think could have been done differently to avoid this problem?

_____

_____

2 Which steps did the sous chef disregard and jeopardize for product quality?

_____

_____

3 How would you explain the situation to the customer?

_____

_____

4 What do you think happened to the standardized recipe of the sauce in the hands of the new cook?

_____

_____

Planning for Quantity Events

Banquet and buffet services are the most profitable area of a hotel; renting out banquet facilities can also be very profitable. However, to ensure profitability and a high level of food quality, quantity events must be well planned. Planning is one of the keys to superior performance and product quality in all areas of food production provided by restaurant and foodservice operations. The need for proper planning is critical for special events such as banquets, **catering**—providing foodservice—and buffets.

A key planning tool for large events is the **Banquet/Buffet Event Order (BEO),** a written contract between the establishment and the customer. It is the main tool to plan the event with the customer and to avoid any surprises. Sometimes called a **function sheet,** the BEO is filled out during the initial interview with the customer and contains all the details about the event—the number of guests expected, the menu, the logistic details, and special needs or requests. Each establishment will have its own specific BEO, but it must contain information as shown in *Exhibit 5e.*

Estimating Customer Count and Booking Events

Most special events require customers to guarantee payment for a specified number of guests. When completing the BEO, it is extremely important to adhere to the organization's minimum and maximum guest requirements and to record the correct guest count. If an incorrect guest count is recorded, then the purchaser will purchase the wrong food quantity, which in turn will cause a number of problems for the kitchen staff to overcome.

If an event is overbooked, there may not be enough food for each guest. To serve everyone in such a situation, the staff might need to cut corners. For example, staff might quickly prepare meals from other available food. Cooks may stretch available food by watering down sauces or by serving only four pieces of asparagus per guest instead of the five that were planned for. In all of these situations, quality might be downgraded and the customer and/or guests might be disappointed by the quality.

If an event is underbooked, the establishment may lose money and have leftover food that was purchased specifically for the event.

Exhibit 5e

Borealis Productions Banquet Event Order

Who and What

Event	Banquet	**Guests**	160	**Date booked**	Oct. 15, 2007		
Sales	Mary Miller	**Site contact**	Brad Babcock	**Contact**	Sean Hinz		
Phone	(313) 555-1217		(313) 555-0819		(313) 555-0714		
Order	#2301						
Customer	Marvin Garfield	**Phone**	(313) 555-3258	**Group**	Family Services Center		

When and Where

Date	July 14	**Day**	Sunday	**Room/s**	Reception in Milky Way Lobby; Dinner in Aurora Room
Times	**Start:** 5:00 p.m.	**Serve:** 6:00 p.m.	**End:** 10:00 p.m.		

Setup notes: One-hour reception with bartender

Foodservice

Menu	Quantity
Standard assorted hors d'oeuvres	4 × 120 pieces
Borealis garden salad	160
Prime NY strip steak #1180, bordelaise sauce	160
Roasted parsley potatoes	160
Steamed asparagus	160 portions
Assorted dinner rolls & butter	175
Standard chocolate mousse	160
Coffee, regular	5 gallons
Decaf	4 gallons
Wine: house red, house white	10 bottles 10 bottles

Staff

Manager:	Mike Sellers
Chef:	Bruno Frank
Cook:	Anna Smith, Eric Ramirez
Setup Helper:	Bryan Hansen, Dave Kapner
Setup Helper:	Cortney Breslan
Bartenders:	Bryan Hansen, Dave Kapner
Waitstaff:	Eric Baltner, Cortney Breslan, Dana Feltzies, Kevin Lopez, Ahmed Mankewicz, Jacqui Nelson, Juan Porter, Ken Pulnetzer, Alex Simmer, Joyce Tempel

Special Requests

Harpist will play at reception from 5 to 6 p.m.
Bar in Milky Way lobby from 5 to 6 p.m.
Set up tables with colored, pressed skirts
10 centerpieces

Comments

Waitstaff to arrive one hour before event to prep tables.

Planning an Event With a Customer

Once the sales director has created an initial BEO with the customer, he or she should review it in detail with the customer. Suggested points to cover are:

- Review each course with the customer and explain it just as you would in a restaurant setting.

- Highlight the product quality, including the grading of meats and origin of product.

- Explain accompaniments, such as starches and vegetables, as clearly as you explain the center of the plate (main protein item).

- Explain the importance of the sauces the chef will use.

- Clarify any special requests, such as vegetarian dishes, food allergies, and other special needs.

- Make beverage and wine recommendations.

Using the BEO in the Back of the House

Once the BEO is finalized with the customer, it will be copied and distributed to all managers involved with the event—the operations manager, restaurant manager, concierge (if in a hotel), and executive chef. Usually these people countersign and return the BEO to the sales manager or person in charge of taking the order. This helps to coordinate an event with the back of the house to ensure product quality. For example, the restaurant manager needs to ensure that special equipment will be on hand for the event. The executive chef needs to ensure that the menu items prepared will meet special requests for vegetarian dishes or avoid certain foods due to food allergies. The key to running a large event smoothly is to follow the event plan.

Avoiding Mistakes

It is critical to plan well—too many things can go wrong if you do not. Some customers may ask your establishment to create dishes that are impossible to create for the setting they want. If you agree to "mission impossible" events for your establishment, you may be setting up your organization for a disaster. Do not be afraid to say "no" to a customer or an event planner if your establishment does not have the experience or capacity to execute the event properly. You can ruin your establishment's hard-earned reputation with one poorly executed event for two hundred and fifty people quicker than you think.

Exhibit 5f provides some examples of what can go wrong if logistical or menu information is gathered incorrectly for a quantity event.

Exhibit 5f

Results of Poor Planning

Problem	Result
Logistic problems	
Inaccurate guest count	Ordering too much or too little food
	Insufficient preparation equipment
	Insufficient preparation time or staff
	Chef may decide to cancel event due to low number of guests
Mix-up of BEOs	Wrong banquet prepared
	Incorrect dish prepared for a buffet
Insufficient information on BEO	Entire course left out of meal
	Not preparing part of a dish; for example, potatoes
	Unable to get specially ordered product
Premises not cleared or cleared incorrectly	On-premises: no room in kitchen for storing supplies, preparing, and serving meal
	On- and off-premises: lack of culinary equipment, lack of production space
	Off-premises: deliveries not accepted, missing outside kitchen equipment, travel issues, sanitation, and garbage disposal
Menu Problems	
Special requests and orders not taken into account	Could cause a major health risk for customer with allergies
	Availability of specialty product not checked before ordering; for example, specialty fish or certain cuts of meat that need longer lead time (time for delivery of ordered product), or long-stemmed strawberries for dipping in chocolate
Menu planning not correct	Courses take too long to serve
	Menu items out of season
	Not able to keep items at correct temperature, especially if off-site
Courses	Courses cannot be executed before or during the event
	Courses cannot be reheated or held to sufficient temperature
Course ingredients	Course consists of too many ingredients
	Ingredients are now out of season or unavailable
Culinary execution	Cooking equipment not available
	Cooks' skill levels not up to needs of menu; training of cooks not possible within time frame available

Working Smartly to Help Events Run Smoothly

On the day of the quantity event, management can use specific tools and techniques to help ensure that the event runs smoothly. Some of these tools and techniques are discussed below.

Use a Production Sheet to Ensure Food Quality

A **production sheet** is a tool used to plan the activities for the day of the event, including items that must be precooked and the quantity needed of each item. (See *Exhibit 5g.*)

Exhibit 5g

Production Sheet for Bakery and Pastry Department

Daily Line Production Baking and Pastry Department for 5/6/07

Item	Amount	Production time	Skill level	FMP signature
Bake pies	9 × 9″ pies	5 min + oven time	☑	
Pastry cream	1 gal	30 min	☑☑	
Pluck fresh mint	50 sprigs for garnish	15 min	☑	
Scoop ice cream for banquet (BEO#34)	100 scoops with purple scoop	30–60 min	☑	
Ice cream production	1 qt for BEO#34	30 min	☑☑	
Prep and bake crème brûlée	48 × 5 oz dishes	45 min	☑☑	
Plate banquet desserts	50 plates for BEO#32	30–45 min		
Bread production	200 rolls	1–4 hr	☑☑	
Meringue	1 gal	15 min	☑☑	
Fruit coulis	1 qt	20 min	☑	
Chocolate mousse	3 gal	40 min	☑☑	
Sugar cookie dough bulk	40 lb	30 min	☑	
Scoop and bake cookies	Purple scoop—100 cookies BEO#32 and BEO# 29	15–30 min	☑	
Pastille flowers for wedding cake	BEO#14	4 hr	☑☑☑	
Sugar showpiece	Special for BEO#14	4+ hr	☑☑☑	
Buttercream	6 gal	30 min	☑☑	
Bake cakes	20 cakes	1 hr oven time	☑☑	
Crème anglaise	1 gal	15 min	☑☑	

Restaurant and foodservice establishments use the production sheet, sometimes called a prep sheet, to ensure that food is of the quality promised. The chef creates the production sheet for the event from the banquet/buffet event order (BEO) to ensure the preparation of enough food and to avoid quality problems during plating or service.

The production sheet is duplicated and used by all prep and line cooks and specific cooks for banquet or buffet applications and other staff in the kitchen. Cooks use this tool to control the conversions of a standardized recipe into the quantity needed to assure a quality outcome for the event. Although the line cook is ultimately responsible for the execution and sufficient production for his or her station, each person should be able to follow the production sheet and to prepare the items at his or her station.

A daily line production sheet for a typical day in a baking and pastry department is shown in *Exhibit 5g.* This sheet compiles all work that must be done and an estimated production time for each item. It does not define what is done first. Usually foodservice employees without experience are responsible for all work on skill level ☑, intermediate foodservice professionals execute work on skill level ☑☑, and the most experienced cooks or the manager work on tasks marked with ☑☑☑. The more employees you have available at an intermediate skill level, the faster you can get high-quality production done.

Responsibilities in the Kitchen

It is important to define roles and responsibilities for each area of the kitchen. This will ensure that the flow of food is efficient and that accidents are avoided. If your staff know what they are responsible for, they are more likely to be successful and your customers will receive the quality product they expect.

The sous chef is generally the person in charge of operations. He or she assigns culinarians to tasks according to their skill level. The more experience the person has, the greater the responsibility for production. The sous chef also needs to consider giving responsibilities to new staff to develop them for greater responsibility.

Line cooks are cooks who have responsibility for cooking for a particular function of the kitchen. Line cooks include sauté cooks, fry cooks, broiler cooks, salad cooks, dessert cooks, garde manger cooks, and any other menu-specific areas (pizza cook, pasta cook, wok cook, etc.). A **garde manger cook** is responsible for the preparation and storage of cold foods such as salads and dressings. Whether assigned to the sauté or dessert station, line cooks must understand the importance of quality food production. Middle- to advanced-level line cooks should be included in developing standard operating procedures (SOPs), such as preparation lists and menu descriptions for banquets and buffets.

Trust the Expediter

An important job on the line is the expediter. The expediter must be a proficient cook—he or she must know all the cooking times and cooking methods for the menu items. When the server places an order for a table, the **expediter** calls out the items in the order in which the cooks need to prepare them, so that meals for a given table are ready for service at the same time and are at the proper temperature. When a cook is asked to **fire** an item—put a protein on the grill—start a pasta sauce, or put a lamb chop in the oven, he or she must work quickly and efficiently. There is no time to explain "why" and "what" during service time. Staff should trust the expediter, execute to the best of their ability, and provide the best quality product they can.

Some establishments have point-of-sale (POS) systems that help the expediter by keeping track of orders fired and picked up, as well as how long customers have been waiting for their food.

Exhibit 5h describes how a meal is prepared for one table, but in an active food establishment, the cooks handle multiple tables, multiple dishes, and multiple tickets. A good memory is key and working fast is imperative to handle the load of information. Not providing the expediter with the dish or item quickly will influence the quality of all the other items and whether they are ready to serve.

Exhibit 5h

The Expediter Places Orders

What the expediter does	What happens in the kitchen
The expediter says, "Ordering for table of 4—item 1, item 2, item 3, item 4."	All cooks must listen and determine whether they are needed for this table and then take actions to prepare for the next step—the firing of the items.
The expediter determines what will take the longest and calls out the items in order of cooking time.	The first fired item will usually be the protein that is the thickest or takes the longest to cook.
If there is no printer that shows dishes are ready, the expediter calls the table number, side dishes, and/or the accompaniments.	Kitchen staff plate main courses and add accompaniments and side dishes.
Expediter calls pickup table.	Plater behind the line puts finishing touches on the plates, garnishes them, cleans them off, and puts them in the window.
Expediter buzzes (electronic pager system) the server for the table. After the meals are picked up, the table ticket/guest check is "stabbed on a needle" for later review or if questions occur.	

Techniques for Precooking Food

Precooking food is a technique to partially cook the food in advance. This process ensures that food is cooked thoroughly while retaining quality and attractiveness. When an order is called, the line cook finishes the cooking.

Most of the techniques cook the food for a short time and usually end by "shocking" the food in cold water to stop the cooking. The food is then drained to keep it dry. The actual firing of the product takes less time than the fresh-cooked version and is as healthy and nutritional as the original product.

These are processes used to partially cook food:

- **Blanch off**—Used frequently on green vegetables and hardy vegetables. Food is trimmed, cleaned, placed in simmering water, and then shocked in cold water to avoid the loss of nutrients.

- **Steam off**—Similar to blanching; however, food is not submerged in liquid, but steamed above water.

- **Partially boil**—Pasta and risotto, which take a long time to cook and require close supervision to prevent overcooking, are partially cooked. When ready to serve, the line cooks finish the cooking. Pasta is partially boiled to a bit under **al dente** (which means "to the bite"). When ready to serve, cooking is finished and the pasta is served with sauce. Risotto is precooked to the last stage, which can be thirty minutes. It is finished in the pan with the remaining ingredients. It is usually stored in a dated bag in the cooler and is portion-controlled.

- **Preparation of bases and sauces**—Sauces and bases for certain dishes are usually prepared in advance. There should always be backup sauces in the cooler to avoid running out of the product. If a kitchen runs out of sauces, chefs might be tempted to cut corners by thinning the sauces to accommodate additional orders.

- **Grill marks**—Chefs prepare meat products for parties or banquets by partially cooking the meat and then making **grill marks**—imprints of the grill—on them. When ready to serve, the meat is fired in the oven.

Activity

One Menu, Many Events

In this activity, consider what needs to be done to offer a current menu item that is sold à la carte for a buffet or banquet event. The restaurant regularly serves one hundred and twenty-five guests per night and has equipment for a menu balanced between grilling, cooking, and deep-frying.

The menu item is based on the six qualities of finished food:

- Appearance
- Temperature
- Aroma
- Texture
- Flavor
- Doneness

Think about the production techniques you have learned. Complete the table below, with the production techniques you would use to retain the quality of the menu item for an à la carte restaurant, banquet for seventy-five to three hundred, or buffet. Keep in mind that when changing from one serving format to another, some parts of the menu may need to be changed. Consider the following questions when determining the techniques you would use:

Storage—Will you need to make special arrangements for a large shipment for a banquet?

Preparing food—How must you store food that has been prepared previously? Will additional storage space be needed? What will need to be precooked? How will precooked items need to be stored? Will additional storage space be needed for precooked items? Will you need extra staff? For which part of the meal might you need extra food at a buffet?

Cooking—Can you cook the food all at one time? What is the best cooking method for each venue? Will some adjustments in the menu need to be made to accommodate batch cooking for a banquet or buffet? If so, for which items?

Holding—Do you need special equipment for holding food?

	À la carte restaurant	Banquet	Buffet
Salmon steak			
Sweet-and-sour sauce			
Grilled mixed vegetables (zucchini, eggplant, and onions)			
Fried sweet potato curls			
Garnish: sliced daikon, which must be iced, sprinkled with black sesame seeds			

Summary

In this chapter, you learned about ways to prepare food to preserve quality in large-scale production. You learned the differences between the three types of foodservice: à la carte restaurant service, sometimes called full-service dining; banquets; and buffets. Sometimes a recipe that is very successful at an à la carte restaurant needs to be modified to be served at a banquet. Ingredients, preparation, and cooking methods also may need adjustments.

When planning a banquet event, either on-premises or off-premises, managers use a Banquet/Buffet Event Order (BEO) to plan the food and logistics. The BEO is copied and used by all people involved in the event.

The other key tool to successful production for a banquet or buffet is the production sheet. The production sheet spells out the amounts of food and the production time needed. The production sheet is similar to the preparation sheet at an à la carte restaurant.

Quantity production is one of the greatest challenges to people working in the restaurant and foodservice industry. It is also one of the most rewarding aspects to see a successful event carried out to perfection.

Review Your Learning

1 Who is *not* a part of the line crew?

 A. Executive chef

 B. Expediter

 C. Grill cook

 D. Sauté cook

2 The most preferred skill to have as a line cook is

 A. being a fast cook.

 B. reading culinary magazines.

 C. following quality food production standards.

 D. being able to estimate measurements.

3 A production sheet is *not* used for

 A. converting standardized recipes.

 B. reviewing what has to be done for this shift.

 C. ordering from a vendor.

 D. controlling who is doing what and how quickly.

4 The expediter during a busy shift is probably going to be the

 A. buser.

 B. sous chef.

 C. sauté cook.

 D. server.

5 What is the main factor to consider when determining whether you can execute an in-house catering event?

 A. Suitable menu

 B. Kitchen capacity

 C. Amount of kitchen staff you will need

 D. Amount of seats you have available

6 A Banquet/Buffet Event Order (BEO) is similar in function to what other document?

 A. Function sheet

 B. Standardized recipe

 C. Order book

 D. Production sheet

7 When writing a prep sheet, what is *not* important to include?

 A. Name of the plate the item goes on

 B. Quantity

 C. Name of the product

 D. Signature of the manager

8 If you have to travel with ready-to-eat food to a catering site, what is the most important factor to have?

 A. Enough service utensils

 B. Enough cooling units at the site

 C. A fast driver

 D. Safe food transportation

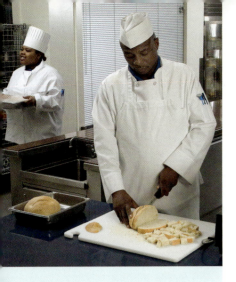

6

Is There Food Quality in Leftover Food?

Inside This Chapter

- A Systematic Approach to Repurposing Food
- Options for Repurposing Food
- Ensuring Safety When Repurposing Food
- Ensuring Quality When Repurposing Food
- Ethical Considerations When Repurposing Food

After completing this chapter, you should be able to:

- Use a systematic approach when working with quality leftovers.
- Give examples of safely repurposed food.
- Describe general procedures for safely repurposing food.
- Describe ways to maintain quality in repurposed food.

Test Your Knowledge

1 **True or False:** Bread can be reused if it is removed from a customer's table and has not been touched. *(See p. 117.)*

2 **True or False:** It is allowable for cooks and service staff to eat food that is returned on a cart from a buffet reception. *(See p. 124.)*

3 **True or False:** A party of twelve has just cancelled a dinner reservation. There are additional vegetables for the party that have been blanched to save time. It is acceptable and safe to reuse them. *(See p. 117.)*

4 **True or False:** A kitchen is a controlled environment; the customer eating area is controllable as well. *(See p. 117.)*

5 **True or False:** It is acceptable to reuse thirty steamed fish portions left over from a buffet for an event the following day. *(See p. 118.)*

Key Terms

Color-coded, food rotation label

Controlled environment

Cross-contamination

Food rescue program

Repurposed food

Time-temperature abuse

Introduction

Although the same food safety principles apply to all types of restaurant and foodservice establishments, the opportunities for repurposing food depend on the type of operation involved.

Hotels, for example, can have countless opportunities to reuse food. Depending on their size, hotels can hold up to one hundred or more food-related events, banquets, or buffets on a single day. For example, a hotel can hold a cookie-and-drink break for a small meeting and at the same time, handle an eight-course meal for 175 people.

Banquet chefs are responsible for meeting budgeted food costs while ensuring that the food is high quality and safe for all types of events. But what happens if guests do not show up? What if, after an event, the chef realizes that there is a leftover pan of steamed broccoli?

Some institutions never consider reusing food. Many national restaurant chains have standards of throwing out food that is not used within a half-hour of cooking. Airlines and other institutions discard food if it is not served within a specified time limit.

No matter what the circumstances, as the manager, it is important for you to ensure that your staff follow the guidelines for repurposing food described in this chapter.

Think About It...

Hot dogs and other types of sausages were originally made out of leftovers. Think of other popular dishes that were created from leftovers.

A Systematic Approach to Repurposing Food

Repurposed food is food that was not consumed by customers, but was prepared, cooked, cooled, and held safely in a controlled environment, such as a kitchen. Most of the time, repurposed food is food that was prepared in advance for customers but not served; therefore, the product was not yet paid for.

Safety and quality are obviously the key components to which you must pay scrupulous attention. *Exhibit 6a* on the next page shows a decision tree containing questions that will aid you in deciding whether or not to repurpose food.

Basically, there are two key questions that must be asked in order to determine whether food can be repurposed:

■ What food is safe to reuse?

■ What options are there for repurposing the food?

Reuse Food Only from a Controlled Environment

To be considered for repurposing, food must have been prepared and held in a controlled environment. A **controlled environment** is one in which food has been within the kitchen's control and has been kept safe from cross-contamination and time-temperature abuse. **Cross-contamination** occurs when microorganisms are transferred from one food or surface to another. A controlled environment is also one in which food is safe from biological, chemical, or physical hazards and personal hygiene issues. Food should be in a controlled environment from the time it is received until it reaches the customer. As soon as a dish leaves the server's tray, the dish is out of the controlled environment of the food production area.

Once food is on a customer's table, it cannot be reused. Think about some situations that are out of the control of any restaurant employee and could cause contamination. Would you want to eat food under any of the following circumstances?

■ A customer touches bread and puts it back in the basket.

■ A customer coughs on a plate of food, and then returns it to the kitchen.

Exhibit 6a

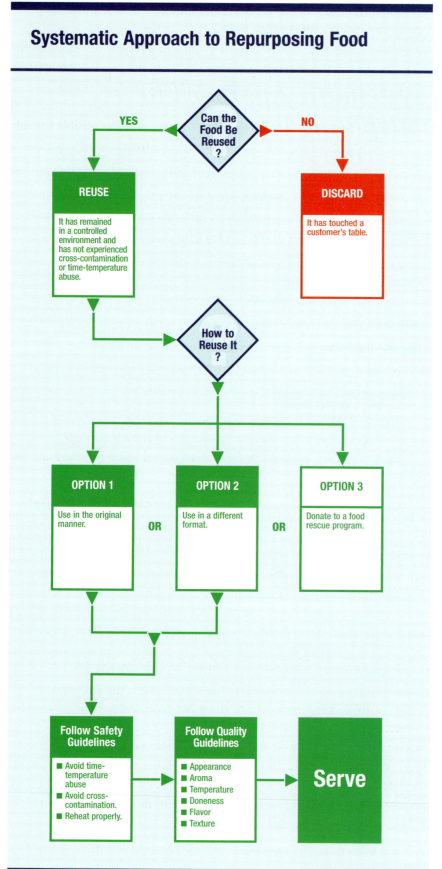

Systematic Approach to Repurposing Food

- A customer sneezes into her napkin, which she later drapes over the untouched bread basket. A busser, not realizing this, takes the basket back to the kitchen.

- People are hovering over a sweets table at a buffet or banquet.

All these situations could result in contaminated or unsafe food. Any food that touches the customer, whether at a single table, buffet, or banquet table, should never find its way back to the production kitchen but should be thrown out immediately.

In addition, food that has been held at unsafe temperatures for too long must also be discarded, as it has experienced **time-temperature abuse.**

Options for Repurposing Food

As shown on the system diagram in *Exhibit 6a*, there are three ways to reuse food—two of them within a food enterprise.

1. Food can be served in its original format.

2. Food can be repurposed into another format. For example, chicken that has been in a controlled environment may be reused in chicken salad.

3 Food can be donated to local food rescue programs, which are located in many communities. These **food rescue programs** are nonprofit organizations that obtain mainly prepared and perishable food items from food establishments and distribute them to local food banks or soup kitchens, which, in turn, distribute the items to individuals and families. Food banks have a similar operation, but they collect and distribute primarily nonperishable food. Your restaurant or foodservice operation is responsible for safe handling of the food before it is accepted by the rescue program.

Follow these guidelines when donating food to a food rescue program:

- Work with the food rescue program to determine what food it will accept. As a general rule, food rescue programs will only accept unserved food that can be safely transported and reused and will not accept foods that spoil easily.

- Work with the food rescue program to determine who will transport the food. Most programs offer free pickup of food and have employees and volunteers who have been trained in safe food handling procedures.

- Ensure that the food you wish to donate is within the expiration date and has not been time-temperature abused.

- Package the food as the food rescue program requests. Many programs request that food be packaged in reusable airtight containers. Also ensure that food is packaged in such as way as to prevent leakage and cross contamination.

- Store the food at the correct temperature (below 40°F [4.4°C] or above 140°F [60°C]). If food is to be picked up late in the day or the next morning, cool down and refrigerate or freeze any heated leftovers.

- Check the food for signs of spoilage.

Examples of Repurposed Food

Once you know that a food item is eligible for reuse, you need to consider other factors when repurposing it.

Different food items are potentially more hazardous than others when reused. Some kitchen conditions present more potential hazards for reused food. *Exhibit 6b* on the next page shows examples of various food products, potential hazard levels, and other conditions that affect the safety of the unused food. The table includes recommended actions for using each product listed. The last column describes what you should never do when reusing a food item.

Exhibit 6b

Evaluating Food for Repurposing

Product	Current State of the Product	Potential Hazard Level
White bread	Covered, in drying rack.	Low
Beef barley soup	Cooled safely (soup and garnish separated); labeled in cooler.	Low
Cream horns filled with stabilized, vanilla-flavored heavy cream filling	Stored in pastry department cooler and labeled.	Low
Fully cooked prime rib (medium rare)	Not served; cooled safely after cooking; labeled and stored in cooler.	Low
Grilled chicken breast	Left over from warmer in back of the house during lunchtime. Placed in a cooler immediately from warmer.	High
Green leaf salad	Held in cooler.	Low
Baked potatoes	Held at 140°F (60°C) for four hours; cooled safely; foil removed.	Low
Fresh orange juice	Kept during service hours in the cooler.	Low
Gravy from convenience product	Held during service above 135°F (57°C).	Low
Pulled BBQ pork	Held on a service line for four hours at a temperature of 140°F (60°C) and then cooled to 52°F (11°C) and placed into the cooler.	High
Sauces for the line (containing potentially hazardous ingredients)	Cooled safely; then labeled and stored at 41°F (5°C).	Low

Options for Reuse	Don'ts
Make into breadcrumbs.	Do not keep it in the cooler or on the counter until someone buys it.
Reheat soup to the proper temperature for reuse and cool down safely as many times as needed, as long as the reheating and cooling are done correctly. Evaluate garnish for quality; reuse or make fresh.	Although properly reheating and cooling soup multiple times is permitted, quality will suffer each time the soup goes through this process. Therefore, check quality each time.
Serve within two days. Check taste of filling for quality.	Do not freeze and reuse because filling will separate and dough will be chewy.
Reheat in pieces for immediate service or slice for sandwiches.	Do not reheat pieces more than once for quality. If sliced beef is kept too long, it spoils or dries out.
None.	Do not reuse since the chicken has not been cooled properly.
Use same day; otherwise, it will wilt.	Do not keep it on the counter or in the cooler too long.
Cut, scoop out, deep-fry the next day for potato skins. Make sure to remove foil.	Do not leave foil on, since foil can cause botulism.
Taste product the next day before service. If product seems okay, use the same way as day before.	Do not leave fresh juices out on the bar. Keep container and pouring spout clean.
Reuse within seven days. Must reheat to proper temperature if held for use.	Do not use after seven days.
None.	Do not reuse food that has been time-temperature abused. Discard it.
Reuse, if reheated to 165°F (74°C) for fifteen seconds within two hours of initial cooking.	Do not reheat more than once for quality reasons.

Ensuring Safety When Repurposing Food

Food safety must be the first and primary concern when repurposing food, especially in the cooling and reheating phases.

Each step in the preparation and handling of food presents potential hazards. If food is prepared and/or cooked properly, held at the proper temperature, cooled down properly, labeled correctly, and stored correctly—but reheated incorrectly—then the food is no longer reusable.

This section provides you with guidelines to follow when reusing food. Note that at each stage it is important to document the entire holding, cooling, and reheating process.

Avoid Time-Temperature Abuse

The most important rule is to avoid time-temperature abuse of food that is potentially hazardous. Potentially hazardous food is food that must remain in time-temperature control in order to remain safe. These types of food typically allow harmful microorganisms to grow quickly. Potentially hazardous food items can be abused if they are held in the temperature danger zone of 41°F (5°C) to 135°F (57°C) for more than four hours. Since time-temperature abuse can result in the growth of disease-causing microorganisms, be sure to follow the storage procedures found on the specification sheet for each item. If food products are time-temperature abused, they must be discarded.

Label Products Correctly

Proper labeling is especially important for food that is being repurposed. Proper labeling should include the date and time the food was produced, who produced it, and when to discard it. In a **color-coded, food rotation label** system, a colored sticker is placed on food before it is refrigerated. The key to this system is the color code on the label for each day of the week. Institutions typically use the colored labels to indicate which day a food item was stored in the cooler; however, some restaurants and foodservice establishments may use the labels to tell the last day a food product should be used. Whatever system is used, the label indicates which food should be used first, following the first in, first out (FIFO) rule. (See Chapter 3 for more information on receiving and storage.)

Control Food During Holding, Cooling, Storing, and Reheating

Whether food is being prepared for the first time or being repurposed, it is critical from a safety perspective to keep it controlled during holding, cooling, and storage. Time-temperature abuse must be avoided at all costs. In addition, care must be taken to prevent cross-contamination between fully cooked and raw items. One way of accomplishing this is to immediately vacuum seal (seal without air in a plastic bag) food, preventing cross-contamination from occurring.

Follow proper reheating procedures to safely reheat previously cooked food. Food that will be held for service must be reheated to an internal temperature of 165°F (74°C) for fifteen seconds within two hours of initial cooking.

Exhibit 6c

Summary of Quality Guidelines

- Appearance, both of the food and the presentation
- Aroma
- Texture
- Flavor
- Temperature
- Doneness

Ensuring Quality When Repurposing Food

When repurposing food, it is important to follow the quality guidelines described in Chapter 1. (See *Exhibit 6c.*)

One way to ensure quality for leftover food is to use equipment that is known to preserve quality. Some ovens have built-in reheating features. (See *Exhibit 6d.*) Microwave ovens bring the internal temperature of a product to the required standard and retain moisture and flavor. In conventional ovens, the heat comes from a heating element, and there is no air movement. A convection oven uses a fan and gets food hot more quickly, and therefore is preferred to a conventional oven. In many cases, a combination oven will prevent food from being overdried or overcooked during reheating.

Exhibit 6d

Ovens with built-in reheating features.

Photos courtesy of Hobart Corporation

Ethical Considerations When Repurposing Food

In every restaurant or foodservice operation, one of a manager's responsibilities is to keep food cost at the operation's standard. This pressure can pose an ethical dilemma when food is left over from the day's production. It may be tempting to reuse the food rather than to "waste" it by discarding it. Three situations can pose the greatest dilemmas: banquet leftovers, employees' meals, and deliberate overproduction.

After a banquet, food may be unused and remain in a controlled environment. Since there is enough to serve again, it can be tempting to serve the leftover potions to customers rather than "wasting" the food. However, most banquet and catering contracts specify that food prepared for the event may not be used again. Ethical managers will honor the terms of the contract and dispose of the leftover food.

Some establishments offer meals to employees. Ethical managers maintain the same sanitation and quality standards for employees as they do for customers. If the quality of a food item drops to a point at which you would not serve it to customers, then do not serve it to your employees either. If your establishment charges staff for employee meals, make sure the meals are fresh, nutritional, and include a variety of offerings.

Although repurposing is a legitimate use of leftover food, a restaurant or foodservice operation should not deliberately overproduce food just to repurpose it in other recipes. If an establishment finds that it is often repurposing food, then the standardized recipes or production quantities must be changed.

In repurposing leftover food, as in all other aspects of restaurant and foodservice operation, management must act ethically.

Activity

Use It or Lose It!

Here are three situations in which you must decide what to do about food that has not been consumed. Read the situations and then answer the questions.

Wedding Party

A wedding party has booked a reservation for 300 people, but only 250 guests attend the dinner. You have already cooked the prime rib for this event. The prime rib never left the kitchen and is being held in a warming unit in a safe food environment of 140°F (60°C).

1 Is it safe to serve the remaining fifty portions of prime rib to customers?

_____

2 Is it acceptable to charge a second customer for the prime rib dinners that have already been paid for?

_____

The Bakery

A bakery produces cinnamon rolls every morning at 4:00 a.m. for the breakfast crowd. The par level on the prep sheet for production is accurate, and there are generally no leftovers. From time to time, though, there have been unsold rolls. On days when the weather is bad, fewer customers come in for their coffee and breakfast. Occasionally, the police or fire department has an emergency and is unable to pick up its usual order of cinnamon rolls.

One day, the staff realized that the bakery could grind the leftover rolls into streusel—a crumbly mix of sugar, flour, butter, cinnamon, and sometimes nuts—to use on top of coffeecakes. The bakery benefitted by doing this because they started selling more coffeecakes when they switched from purchased to homemade streusel. Today, the bakery produces enough cinnamon rolls to serve all of their customers and also make streusel.

1 What happened to the bakery's food production and quality?

_____

_____

2 What do you think happened financially?

_____

_____

3 What else can streusel be used for in a bakery setting?

_____

_____

continued on next page

Use It or Lose It! *continued from previous page*

Winter Dinner

One January day, the executive chef of a restaurant prepared baked ham as an evening special. He expected to sell forty servings. Unfortunately, the weather was bad that night and the restaurant only sold five servings, leaving thirty-five leftover portions. The chef had prepared the ham according to a standardized recipe, following proper food safety procedures.

Because of the bad weather, the line cook started cleaning up early. He unplugged the warming unit three hours before closing.

The sous chef did not realize that the warming unit had been unplugged when he told the executive chef, "I will take care of the ham." The executive chef understood the sous chef to mean that he would discard the ham. However, the sous chef put the ham in the refrigerator because he was planning to serve the cold ham in sandwiches to the employees the next day.

1 Was the ham safe to repurpose and serve to the employees the next day? Why or why not?

_____

_____

2 What could have been done differently?

_____

_____

Summary

There is a system to safely reuse food. First, the chef must decide if the food has remained in a controlled environment. If it has not, then the chef must immediately discard the food. If it has, then the chef can consider options for repurposing the food.

There are three options for reusing food. The food may be repurposed within the operation by serving the food in the same manner as the original format, or it may be repurposed by serving it in a different format. Another option would be to donate the food to a local food rescue program that distributes food to shelters.

When food is repurposed within an enterprise, it is imperative to follow proper food safety guidelines. Additional monitoring must occur for repurposed food, and quality should never be compromised.

Other considerations for repurposing food involve ethics, such as serving lower-quality, repurposed food to employees, or serving leftover food that was not used by a first party to a second party. A different management issue may arise if a restaurant or foodservice operation continually uses repurposed food.

Review Your Learning

1 Which equipment is preferred for safely reheating reusable food?

A. 450°F (232°C) conventional oven

B. 125°F (52°C) convection oven

C. Microwave

D. Charbroiler

2 Which is a positive quality standard of a usable leftover product?

A. Freezer burn

B. Product was not covered and is completely dried out

C. Product was not labeled in the cooler

D. Product was held in a controlled environment

3 Which factor does *not* ensure the safety of repurposed food?

A. Correct labeling

B. Tasting the product

C. Checking temperature during cooling

D. Storing at an appropriate temperature

4 Which action is *not* recommended in repurposing food?

A. Properly cooling food and reheating it once for use

B. Reheating, cooling, and serving food over the week until it is gone

C. Using food for an employee meal

D. Donating food to a food rescue program

5 Which reason for leftover food will *not* occur if staff follows standard operating procedures?

A. Fewer customers than forecast

B. Cancellation of parties on short notice

C. Too much food prepared and cooked

D. Weather influence

6 Which information on a label is *not* important when storing reusable food?

A. Time when it was first stored

B. Name of the product

C. Name of the party for which it was used

D. Date when it was stored

7 Where does the controlled environment stop?

A. The restaurant bar

B. The kitchen window

C. When food leaves the server's tray

D. The customer's fork

8 Which use is acceptable for repurposing cooked food?

A. Donating it to a food rescue program

B. Serving it in its original manner

C. Using it as an ingredient in another menu item

D. All of the above

Notes

Building a Quality System

7

Inside This Chapter

- Creating a Quality System
- Assessing and Maintaining Your Professional Skills

After completing this chapter, you should be able to:

- Describe a system that helps to monitor and maintain quality.
- Explain the skills needed for quality food production using the professional skills matrix.
- Assess your own quality management skills.

Test Your Knowledge

1 **True or False:** Quality standards, once in place, do not need to be monitored. (*See p. 131.*)

2 **True or False:** All the skills needed in a food production setting are of equal importance. (*See p. 146.*)

3 **True or False:** Menu items are spotchecked only when new. (*See p. 143.*)

4 **True or False:** Resolving problems is the responsibility of the manager. (*See p. 137.*)

5 **True or False:** Deviations in quality are noted the day they occur. (*See pp. 133–135.*)

Key Terms

Deviation   Root cause

Quality system   Spotchecking

Introduction

A successful restaurant or foodservice operation must maintain a high level of quality at all times. To accomplish this, establishments must have a system in place to build and maintain quality. Implementing quality is an ongoing process. Since there are many components to a good meal—top ingredients, preparation, cooking, and serving—it is a challenge to maintain quality at all times. An operation should use a system to ensure that quality is monitored regularly, rather than only reacting to problems brought to its attention by customers.

Restaurant and foodservice professionals need a high level of skill to consistently monitor food quality and implement quality processes. Therefore, skill growth is required for professional development in:

1 Preparing for jobs with increasing responsibility.

2 Maintaining quality in the establishment where you are employed.

The Professional Skills Matrix in this chapter, as shown in *Exhibit 7h* on p. 146, is a tool that has several applications. It shows the relation of a skill to the work in any kitchen. Use this tool to learn about the key skills that a restaurant or foodservice professional must possess. You will also learn to use it as a self-assessment tool to promote career growth.

Creating a Quality System

Most problems in a restaurant or foodservice operation occur because, during busy meal times, employees forget to do things, take shortcuts, or make other minor mistakes. Usually, other employees compensate and correct these gaps before they reach the customers' tables. If these gaps are ignored and not corrected, however, they can become big problems. It is important to have a system to regularly review operations so that gaps do not occur. Everyone must be part of the system in order for it to work.

A **quality system** outlines how quality processes and procedures should be implemented, controlled, and maintained. It involves the steps listed and illustrated in *Exhibit 7a*.

Exhibit 7a

Quality System Overview

1 | Set criteria
■ Food production
■ Food quality

5 **Maintain**
■ Regularly reevaluate

Quality in an Operation

2 **Identify deviations**
■ Each meal, daily, weekly

4 **Make corrections**
■ All staff involved

3 **Determine causes**
■ In flow of food
■ Outside flow

1 **Set criteria.** Determine the standards for food quality, food production, and service against which you will evaluate all products served to customers.

2 **Identify deviations.** Monitor and inspect all products served to customers. Identify those that do not meet standards.

3 **Determine cause(s).** Determine why the deviation in quality has occurred.

4 **Make corrections.** Figure out what to do; communicate to staff (up and down) and then fix the problem, including training if necessary.

5 **Maintain.** Regularly verify that the standards are being maintained.

Set Criteria

As you learned in Chapter 1, restaurant or foodservice operations use four primary standards (see *Exhibit 7b*):

■ Product specification sheets

■ Preparation sheets

■ Standardized recipes

■ Menu descriptions

These standards are the criteria against which management compares food items and declares them acceptable or unacceptable.

Exhibit 7b

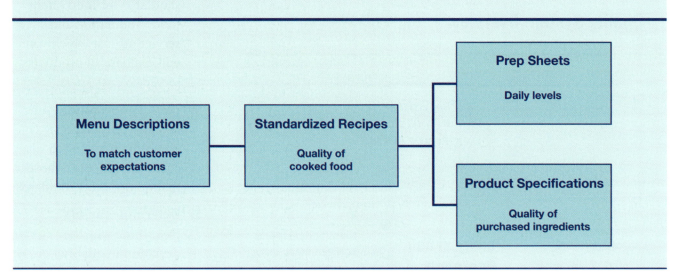

Criteria for Quality Food

Menu Descriptions — To match customer expectations

Standardized Recipes — Quality of cooked food

Prep Sheets — Daily levels

Product Specifications — Quality of purchased ingredients

Product Specification Sheets

Following a standardized recipe does not ensure by itself the appropriate level of quality. Chefs must use ingredients of appropriate quality when executing the recipe. Product specification sheets, or spec sheets, are the main tools for communicating desired ingredient quality to suppliers. In addition, the operation's receiving clerk must use spec sheets to determine if a supplier's goods meet the desired standards of the operation.

Preparation Sheets

Preparation sheets, or prep sheets, are the standards for daily levels of the basic items needed to execute the menu items that day. The prep sheets specify the par levels of the basic items so that no substitutions or last-minute preparations will be needed.

Standardized Recipes

Standardized recipes are the standards against which management judges the quality of the prepared and cooked food. Since standardized recipes specify the exact ingredients, ingredient amounts, and methods for preparing a food item, they help to ensure that each chef will prepare the item in exactly the same way each time and that the resulting item will meet the chef's standards for:

- Aroma
- Texture
- Appearance
- Doneness
- Temperature
- Flavor

Menu Descriptions

Menu descriptions are the standards against which the quality of the fully prepared and served menu items are judged. On the menu, descriptions guide customers' ordering decisions and set their expectations. More detailed menu descriptions increase a server's knowledge of the menu items and act as a guide to proper plating and presentation. According to the National Restaurant Association's Accuracy in Menu Guidelines published in 1984, the menu description should match what is actually served in terms of quantity, quality, product identification, points of origin, and use of brand names.

When food is served, staff, customers, and sometimes food critics determine whether the food meets the standards implied in the menu description.

Identify Deviations

Things do not always go as planned, however. Patrons come at different hours than expected, weather keeps people away, or food is not available from vendors as you expect. It is hard to follow precisely all the steps in the flow of food in the hectic pace of the kitchen. Therefore, **deviations,** or differences from the established standards, are likely to occur. Operations identify deviations in food products by regularly monitoring them—from their receipt from the supplier to their service at the customer's table. Therefore, identifying deviations in food products involves everyone in the establishment. When employees identify deviations, they must track them so that suitable solutions to the deviations can be found. There are four steps in identifying and tracking deviations:

1. Monitor food production.
2. Inspect each dish that is served.
3. Track daily deviations.
4. Review product deviations weekly.

Monitor Food Production

Quality deviations can occur before and during production. Food managers should work with all staff in the back of the house to be sure that any deviations in uncooked products are detected and do not move to the next phase in production.

- **Monitor before, during, and after food products come through the door.** Quality can be preserved during receiving and storage. Mistakes made here jeopardize the whole flow of food—accepting a product not up to the specifications, or damaging a product during receiving or storage will cause an unacceptable product on the customer's table, if not caught early and stopped.

- **Prevent deviations during preparation.** The preparation stage of the process is carried out by beginning-level employees. They are not likely to damage food products, but food can lose its quality if beginners do not work quickly. Yield and portion control can be affected and long food preparation times can cause food to exceed the time-temperature abuse range. These deviations can cause additional expense if food must be discarded and can also cause a chain reaction of problems up to the time the customer's dish is served.

- **Monitor dishes during cooking.** During the cooking process, employees should look for deviations and be supervised by restaurant or foodservice management professionals. Conversion mistakes, a cook's personal creativity, cutting corners, and misreading or not understanding standardized recipes can all cause deviations.

Inspect Each Dish That Is Served

Each time a dish is ready to leave the kitchen, it should be inspected for quality. Obviously, the best time to resolve a problem is before a customer notices. Both food prep and serving staff are responsible for evaluating a finished dish before it reaches a customer.

Visual evaluation before serving a dish catches problems that can be corrected easily, such as a lack of garnish or a dish that has not been held at a specified serving temperature. Another reason visual evaluation is important is that it is usually the first clue that there may be a larger problem to be solved. Menu descriptions can be especially helpful with this issue.

Track Daily Deviations

Obviously, taking notes each time a person notices a deviation is not practical in a busy kitchen at mealtime. It is important, however, at the end of each shift or at the end of the day, depending on the structure of the enterprise, to ask people to recall any problems or deviations that occurred during the shift and how the problems were resolved. The manager should record the information on the Daily Note Sheet, as shown in *Exhibit 7c*. Notes in the Suggestions column do not always need to be extensive.

Exhibit 7c

Daily Note Sheet

Chef on duty/manager on duty: _____ Date: _____ Shift: _____

Day of week: _____

Circumstances to note (weather, special event, etc.) _____

By whom	Item noted	Time	Deviation, problem	Resolution	Suggestions
BN	No garnish on Grilled Salmon	6:15 p.m.	Parsley not in dish	Prep cook to get parsley from storage, put in garnish tray	Have more parsley on hand before shift starts
AL	NY Steak not steaming	6:30 p.m.	Finished too early	Refired it	
BN	No garnish on soup of the day	6:40 p.m.	Ran out of garnish (crackers)	Used garnish from special soup	Higher par level for garnish

Once the manager reviews the Daily Note Sheet, it is a good idea to incorporate the results into the next day's preshift meeting. Sharing the results regularly brings three things to the staff's attention:

■ Tracking deviations is an ongoing process.

■ Discussing the deviations can identify potential problems.

■ Solving problems is everyone's business.

Retain the Daily Note Sheets for a long enough period so that weekly evaluations can be made and patterns of deviations can be noted. This is also necessary because some establishments may have specials for a week, others for only a day. Deviations are to be noted even for specials in order to improve performance and ensure the highest quality for the customer.

Review Product Deviations Weekly

The main purpose of the Weekly Review, as shown in *Exhibit 7d*, is to consolidate information in order to detect patterns of problems so staff can stop them before they become larger issues. Management should incorporate the Daily Note Sheets into the Weekly Review of Product Deviations. Weekly summaries give a perspective on the past week. Be sure to note special circumstances, such as holidays, or whether the food establishment held a special event or banquet.

Review all Daily Note Sheets for the week and summarize them into the Weekly Review of Product Deviations form. Be sure to incorporate the suggestions from the Daily Note Sheets into the "Suggestions" column of the Weekly Review of Product Deviations.

The key to identifying deviations is regular monitoring and understanding by the staff that it is the responsibility of everyone in the establishment. Constantly monitoring food quality is not difficult to do, but it may take time to turn it into a habit for everyone. It is also essential that all staff—management, the executive chef, waitstaff, front-of-the-house staff, and kitchen staff—are involved and that their opinions are considered and valued.

Exhibit 7d

Weekly Review of Product Deviations

Manager   W/E

Items being evaluated

Special events

Profile of standard (description and photo, if appropriate)

Description of dish being evaluated (photo, if appropriate)

Item	# times	Deviation	Resolution	Possible reason	Suggestions
Sweet/sour chicken	1 @ M, W, Th	Overdone meat, as well as fruits	Cooked shorter time	■ Left in too long ■ Oven too hot	■ Calibrate oven ■ Change sauce consistency
Dessert					
Salad					

Determine Root Causes of Problems

It is important to discover the **root cause,** or the true cause of a problem. Naming something as the root cause without careful investigation occurs frequently. However, identifying the wrong item as the root cause may slow down the improvement of a situation.

The problem may be due to something within the kitchen or something outside the kitchen's direct control. Most problems occur when people skip steps as they work. If there is no penalty for an error the first time, the mistake is likely to be repeated.

A method to identify the root cause of a problem is to ask a set of common questions for each noted deviation. Using such questions builds two important characteristics into the process of analyzing root causes:

- **Consistency**—Staff will get into the pattern of looking for deviations using the same questions and patterns.

- **Objectivity**—The questions do not blame anyone. The same questions are asked each time a problem, or potential problem, is discovered.

Once a set of deviations is identified as a problem, the entire staff need to find the cause. Use the Problem-Solving Worksheet as shown in *Exhibit 7e* on the next page to help.

The Problem-Solving Worksheet is arranged in the order of the flow of food. Asking the questions in the "Possible problem" column will help pinpoint causes. The "Other possible problems" column should be completed with information that was identified by the questions in the "Possible problem" column and information from the Daily Note Sheet.

Example of Using the Problem-Solving Worksheet

This is an example of a problem in which the root cause was unexpected. Astute observation combined with problem solving helped resolve an expensive problem for the restaurant.

"I was the executive sous chef in an upscale white tablecloth American cuisine restaurant. We served highly graded steaks. High-quality seafood was flown in daily from Boston. We had a major problem, however, as customers told us again and again that the food was served cold. The chef and owner were investigating this problem: one blamed it on the kitchen, the other on the service staff. We also tried having bussers bring the food to the table for the waitstaff to serve to the customers, but even then the food would be lukewarm. The servers were stumped as well.

Think About It...

As you are learning, the problem you see may not be the root cause of a problem in an operation. Think about situations in which you were surprised about the true cause of a problem. Share with others in your class.

Exhibit 7e

Problem-Solving Worksheet

Manager _____   W/E _____

Items being evaluated _____

Special events _____

Profile of standard (description and photo, if appropriate) _____

Description of dish being evaluated (photo, if appropriate) _____

Category	Possible problem	Other possible problems
Purchasing	■ Has product quality from vendor changed? ■ Is there a new vendor?	
Receiving	■ Was a food safety check made? ■ Was a quality check executed? ■ Is there a deviation from the spec sheet?	
Storage	■ Were food safety procedures checked? ■ Was FIFO followed?	
Preparation	■ Was a yield test performed per spec sheet? ■ Was the standardized recipe used? ■ Were foodservice employees trained on this item?	
Cooking	■ Are problems with one item in dish? ■ Has equipment changed or been recalibrated? ■ Are all tools available?	
Holding, cooling, reheating	■ Is all equipment operational? ■ Was equipment temperature checked? ■ Was a time-temperature abuse check performed?	
Serving	■ Is service timing adequate? (Servers must be paced to customers' orders.) ■ Are plate covers used? ■ Is seating turnover rate too high to serve food promptly?	
Staffing	■ Do staff understand the SOPs? ■ Have staffing levels changed? ■ Is there new staff?	
Other considerations	■ Did anything unusual occur during the time the problem occurred? Holiday, large event, weather, etc.? ■ Have there been environmental changes (AC, heat, etc.) in the kitchen, restaurant, service area?	

We systematically went through the list of questions on the Problem-Solving Worksheet. Since the food was already prepared, we considered questions only in the last four categories: Holding, Serving, Staffing, and Other Considerations.

One day I was working the front of the house, calling out tickets and putting together trays, and I realized that the cold take-up air in the heating system was blowing on the food from above. Every single tray of hot food was getting blasted with ice-cold air from the take-up vent. I assumed this was the root cause of the problem and suggested getting plate covers for the dishes. The plate covers did the trick—they kept the cold air from cooling off the hot food."

Using the problem-solving worksheet helped the executive sous chef identify the category of the problem. Once he knew that the problem was outside of the kitchen, he became a detective. When he felt the cool air, he realized what was causing the problem.

Activity

Identifying Possible Causes of Problems

Review the problems below. For each problem, underline the words that indicate an issue with quality. Use the Problem-Solving Worksheet to help you identify possible problems. Write at least two possible causes on the lines below the problem. Discuss the resolutions with the class.

1 Convenience sauce on the center of the plate is lumpy and does not taste as it should.

_____

_____

_____

2 In the window on the line, mashed potatoes are cold, but the meat on the dish is the perfect temperature.

_____

_____

_____

3 A quick-service restaurant has problems with the fries always being too cold, while the burger is the perfect temperature.

_____

_____

_____

continued on next page

Identifying Possible Causes of Problems *continued from previous page*

4 In an Italian family restaurant, the pasta is overcooked, but the shrimp in the pasta sauce is still not done.

_____

_____

5 The cheese on each bowl of French onion soup for a buffet of one hundred is burned, but the soup is cold.

_____

_____

6 During an outside catering event for a golf outing, five hundred burgers look well-done, but the lettuce and tomatoes look wilted and not fresh next to the bun.

_____

_____

7 The cake looks great but the inside is still doughy, while the ice cream is in a nice round shape with a mint leaf on top that looks crisp and fresh.

_____

_____

8 The grilled salmon, which was baked until recently, fell apart during grilling in a high-volume lunch establishment. The taste is different as well.

_____

_____

9 The pie crust in a small bakery is not as flaky and tasty as it used to be.

_____

_____

10 A recipe was taken from a small mom-and-pop family diner to be cooked for a large in-house catering event for one thousand people and did not turn out well.

_____

_____

Correct Problems

Once a problem's cause or causes have been discovered, then the manager must work with the entire staff to implement the correction. The problem must be corrected, whether it is caused by a single factor or by multiple factors in several areas of the food establishment. When a problem affects an entire system, it is called a systemic problem. The following actions must be taken:

- **Report the problem to superiors.** Document the problem and the proposed solution. Involve management and supervisors of the areas contributing to the problem.

- **Discuss the problem at a managers' meeting.** For large food chains, this discussion will take place on an internal or regional basis. Some establishments will have to report the issue to the corporate office, and it may take some time to receive an answer.

- **Discuss the problem at the daily staff meetings.** Conduct special meetings if needed. Enlist the staff's cooperation. It may take some time to ensure that all staff agree on the importance of the change so that they will fully cooperate. Whenever possible, put staff in charge of training, maintaining, and implementing changes.

  At the daily meeting, you will probably want to take the following steps:

  1. Review the problem and how you arrived at the root cause.
  2. Explain what needs to be done to correct the problem.
  3. Evaluate any additional staff suggestions, discuss their advantages and disadvantages, and describe the recommended solution.
  4. Demonstrate the correct procedure—if staff have been ignoring standardized recipes, they now need to see the processes done correctly; if there are new procedures, demonstrate them and explain how they may change current procedures.

- **Implement the change.** Incorporate staff in evaluating any new procedures and put staff in charge of training and controlling newly established standardized procedures. Verify that the procedure is being done correctly. Review daily at first, then weekly.

- **Explain in detail what is being done to prevent a recurrence of the problem.** Documenting the new procedures is key.

- **Reevaluate the solution regularly.** If the new procedure does not work, cross-reference its documentation to verify whether the procedure is being carried out as initially implemented. As with any change, it may take a while to ensure that everyone has incorporated it into his or her job. This may involve additional meetings or retraining in specific skills.

Be persistent in following all the steps in this process.

Activity

A Costly Pizza Problem

At a trendy Italian restaurant, there is an appetizer pizza that has been popular for several years. The standardized recipe calls for the pizza to be served cold, cut into twelve equal pieces. The pizza is topped with cream cheese and smoked salmon. The garnish is a dollop of crème fraîche with caviar on all twelve pieces. Lately, the pizza is being served on hot crust, which makes the cream cheese soft and causes the crème fraîche to melt into the smoked salmon—so the presentation is not at all like the menu description. The temperature and texture are incorrect as well. Some servers have mentioned this to the chef and have stopped recommending the once-popular appetizer to customers. Additionally, the general manager has noticed that sales are down for this item. The ingredients—smoked salmon and caviar—make this an expensive loss.

On the following lines write what each person should do to find out the cause of the problem and to correct it.

Server:
_____
_____
_____

General manager:
_____
_____
_____

Chef:
_____
_____
_____

Line cook:
_____
_____
_____

Directions for a role-play:

You have read the situation and written down what each of the four people should do. Now act out how the staff will resolve the situation.

1. Four students should volunteer for each of the four positions.

2. The person acting the role of the server should start.

3. Continue to discuss the situation until the problem is solved.

4. When finished, the class should discuss the roles and the resolution. Is there anything else that should be done?

Maintain Quality: Ongoing Product Evaluation

Products should be evaluated for quality on a regularly scheduled basis. Sometimes product quality deteriorates so slowly that the staff do not notice. Customers, on the other hand, will notice if they have not visited the food establishment for several months. Regularly reviewing standardized recipes and dishes is a way to maintain product quality. This review is referred to as **spotchecking.**

The executive chef plans the spotcheck evaluation with the sous chef. They decide which recipes to test and how to administer the spot check during the shifts. This is not a test of the chef, but how well the standardized recipe is being followed. (See *Exhibit 7f.*) The spotchecking should include the following:

Exhibit 7f

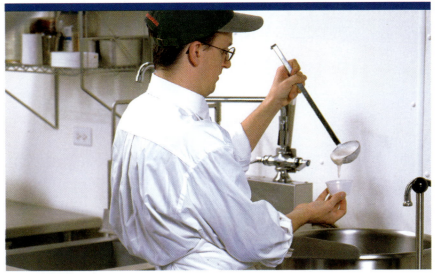

Spotchecking is one way to ensure continued product quality.

- Ordering the same meal from two different shifts using the same server.

- Evaluating the plating, speed, and quality.

- Noticing how well the cook or chef adhered to the standardized recipe.

- Observing the taste and how well it meets your expectations of the finished product.

- Determining whether the meal was the same on both shifts.

You can use an ongoing product evaluation sheet, such as the one shown in *Exhibit 7g* on the next page, to take notes about the meals during the spotcheck.

Plan how to explain the results to the staff, including any changes that will occur as a result of the evaluation. Be sure to explain any problems with the product that were discovered in the evaluation. Include any causes that are outside the kitchen, such as vendors, receiving, substitutions of product, and seasonal changes in product quality.

Exhibit 7g

Ongoing Product Evaluation Sheet

ONGOING PRODUCT EVALUATION

Date _____

Item _____

Evaluator _____

Directions: Order the same item from at least two different shifts. Complete each cell of the table for these factors to be sure that quality is consistent.

Product Checklist	Chef: _____ Shift: _____			Chef: _____ Shift: _____		
	Yes	No	Comments	Yes	No	Comments
Item delivered properly						
Aroma was attractive						
Appearance—plating was attractive, dish was clean						
Dish looks like menu description						
Garnish was correct						
Temperature was correct						
Seasoning was correct						
Flavoring was correct						
Texture was correct						
Doneness was correct						
Other considerations						
Note if substitutions were made and why						
Were any seasonal factors present?						
Other factors						

What changes need to be made? _____

_____

Points to make at preshift meeting _____

_____

Activity

Steakhouse

Read the situation below. Use the Problem-Solving Worksheet on p. 138 to identify the deviation(s) and possible cause(s) and to answer the questions following the situation.

It is a busy Friday night at a steakhouse. You are the manager on the other side of the line—calling out orders, assembling them on the servers' trays, and ensuring that each plate is clean and looks great. In addition, you monitor the cooking to verify great-tasting food.

It is very hectic and there is a full staff. Six cooks are working the line: one on the grill, one on the fryer, two on sauté, another one in the cold kitchen, and one on desserts. The sous chef is also the plater behind the line. Her job is to make sure that all plates are clean and have the correct accompaniments and sauces.

The grill cook on the line puts the plates immediately in the window without listening to your commands for ordering, firing, and picking up. The sous chef must take the plates out of the window to clean them up. She looks at you with a worried face, then brings over a steak dish. You inspect the steak and discover the seventh overcooked steak this evening, a definite sign that the grill cook is overwhelmed and has probably lost his overview of the grill. You immediately ask him if he needs help. He wipes the sweat off his forehead, smiles at you, and denies that he needs help. At the same time, he starts flipping steaks on the 700°F (371°C) wood-fired grill although you have not yet called for more steaks.

1 In which category/categories of the Problem-Solving Worksheet does the problem fall?

_____

_____

2 What is the root cause of the problem?

_____

_____

3 What is your next step as a manager to maintain product quality from the grill with the available staff?

_____

_____

4 Would you serve the steak anyway, in the hope that the customer does not say anything? Remember, you have been buried under tickets all night. A refire or remake of the steak will set you even further back.

_____

_____

Assessing and Maintaining Your Professional Skills

What does it take to become a successful chef or foodservice management professional? Food production, obviously, is one of the basic skills. But other skills are needed as well. The professional skills matrix, as shown in *Exhibit 7h*, describes those skills and the importance of each one.

Exhibit 7h

Professional Skills Matrix

Category	Task	Skills	Importance
General skills	Research	Read and learn about new types of food, equipment, and recipes.	☑☑☑☑
	Mastery of cooking techniques	Proficiently trained on the basics in culinary skills.	☑☑☑
	Creation of new items	Creative; tries new items.	☑☑☑
	Production speed and accuracy	Fast production skills, quick execution of standardized recipes.	☑☑☑☑
Specify quality standards	Ordering	Knowledge of menu, establishment setup, procurement, and products.	☑☑
	Receiving	Product quality knowledge.	☑☑☑
Apply quality standards	Storing	Knowledge of facility and products.	☑☑☑☑
	Preparing	Basic culinary skills.	☑
Implement standards	Cooking	Advanced culinary skills.	☑☑
	From scratch	Experienced culinary skills.	☑
	Flavoring	Experienced culinary skills.	☑☑
	Seasoning	Experienced culinary skills.	☑☑☑
	Accompaniments	Experienced culinary skills.	☑☑☑
	Convenience products	Basic culinary skills.	☑☑
	Plating	Able to combine colors and flavors correctly.	☑☑
Sustain quality standards	Holding	Understand food safety standards. Be able to run holding equipment.	☑
	Cooling	Understand food safety standards. Be able to run cooling equipment.	☑☑☑
Continue quality	Reheating	Understand food safety standards. Be able to run equipment.	☑☑☑☑
	Serving	Understand food safety standards. Monitor food quality.	☑

The Professional Skills Matrix

The Professional Skills Matrix shows the tasks and skills that are needed to be a successful restaurant or foodservice professional, divided by category. Notice the importance column, which indicates how important the tasks are relative to the entire process.

Preparing Yourself: Speed, Practice, and Quality

The realities of cooking for a full house of customers are quite different from preparing courses in culinary training. When the kitchen is at its busiest, you will not have time to figure out what to do. Your actions must be nearly automatic. You will not have time to research or find examples at meal time.

"Practice makes perfect" is an adage that is very true for culinarians. You need to become proficient in many techniques, and to do this you must practice perfecting each part of preparing a meal. Practicing is what any artist or athlete does.

Restaurant or foodservice professionals should start honing their knife skills and practice them every time they are in a lab class or cooking at home for their family. It would surprise an executive chef if a culinary student could cut almost as fast and detailed as he or she could.

For example, in the classroom or even at home, start your production day with a half-hour of cutting practice. Take some low-cost ingredients, select four classic knife cuts, and perform the cuts as quickly and precisely as possible. Always use a ruler or measuring tool to make sure your cut is accurate—speed and accuracy is the goal. Keep track of your measurements and the weight of the finished product, as well as the nonusable waste you produce. Write down these figures each time you practice and keep a log to see your improvement. If you do this exercise every other production day, you will see major improvement in your accuracy and production speed.

Another discipline to master is to maintain quality. Under no circumstances should you ever compromise quality for quantity or speed. Today's customer understands the cooking process and is much more savvy about the proper quality (taste, look, and safe handling) of food. For example, if you change the cut of ingredients, such as switching from a more difficult batonnet cut to a rough cut, customers will notice, since the food will not have the same consistency, and therefore, quality. If you see someone cutting corners in a kitchen, then address it. It is irresponsible for a foodservice professional to let something slide by, knowing that the outcome could lead to an upset customer and possibly a loss of revenue.

Use the Professional Skills Matrix

In addition to practicing your culinary techniques, you will want to increase your skills in the other areas of restaurant and foodservice management. The Professional Skills Matrix provides a listing and rating for each of the most important skills to master. The Professional Skills Matrix can also be used as an assessment tool by rating your current skill level for each task. After rating yourself on each task, you will want to prepare an action plan for increasing your skill levels.

Activity

Assessing Your Skills

Duplicate and use the Professional Skills Matrix (see *Exhibit 7i*) to assess your current skills. In the Current Assessment Column, place one (poor) to four (excellent) check marks to indicate your current level of skill. Ask a peer to rate your current level, using the same scale. In the last column, list the things you need to do to increase each skill. Write your development action plan on the lines below.

Professional Skills Matrix as Self-Assessment

Tasks	Importance	Current Assessment	Peer Assessment	To become more proficient, I need to...
Research	☑☑☑☑			
Mastery of cooking techniques	☑☑☑			
Creation of new items	☑☑☑			
Production speed and accuracy	☑☑☑☑			
Ordering	☑☑			
Receiving	☑☑☑			
Storing	☑☑☑☑			
Preparing	☑			
Cooking	☑☑			
From scratch	☑			
Flavoring	☑☑			
Seasoning	☑☑☑			
Accompaniments	☑☑☑			
Convenience products	☑☑			
Plating	☑☑			
Holding	☑			
Cooling	☑☑☑			
Reheating	☑☑☑☑			
Serving	☑			

Summary

Every restaurant or foodservice operation needs a system to guide it to implement and maintain quality. The system needs to have these components:

1 Set criteria for creating and serving quality food: the standardized recipe, specification sheet, preparation list, and menu description.

2 Identify any deviations from the standards. All staff must look for deviations as each meal is served. The manager should also plan to review any deviations on a daily basis and then summarize these findings weekly. The manager should share the results at daily shift meetings.

3 Involve staff in solving the problems if any are noted. Use the problem-solving worksheet to systematically determine the cause. If hunches are used instead of a system, you might not find the root cause.

4 Correct the problem. Since a serious problem frequently involves many people, involve all staff in implementing the change. Be patient and persistent in making sure that all staff implement the change.

5 Maintain quality by regularly performing spot checks on key items. Your food establishment should have a schedule for doing this regularly.

Quality food production also depends on all staff having superior skills. True restaurant and foodservice management professionals are continually improving their skills and learning about new food, equipment, and industry trends. The Professional Skills Matrix lists the skills that are required and the importance of each in daily work. This is a tool to use in class and throughout your career for professional development. Rate yourself on your proficiency, and then have a colleague or instructor rate your skills. Use the differences to plan ways to improve your skills. The matrix can be used yearly to measure growth.

The pursuit of quality is ongoing. Achieving top quality is one of the major satisfactions of being a restaurant or foodservice manager.

Review Your Learning

1 Which item is *not* part of the criteria set up in a quality system?

A. Product specification sheet

B. Menu description

C. Preparation sheet

D. Quality checklist for finished products

2 Quality criteria are *not* set by the

A. executive chef.

B. manager.

C. line grill staff.

D. sous chef.

3 Which is *not* a cause of product deviations in the kitchen?

A. Creativity of the chef

B. Poor-quality raw ingredients

C. Proper instructions to grill staff

D. Working too fast

4 Managers should discuss deviations from menu descriptions

A. at preshift meetings.

B. at the end of each shift.

C. during meal preparations.

D. each time a dish is served.

5 Using a problem-solving worksheet helps narrow down potential problems because

A. it is important to ask consistent, objective questions.

B. it is important to track all problems.

C. it is impossible to solve problems without the worksheet.

D. None of the above

6 Ongoing product evaluation is important because

A. different chefs can bring their own creativity to recipes.

B. quality can slip without regular spot checks.

C. servers occasionally complain that products do not match menu descriptions.

D. staff changes require additional monitoring.

7 Which task is of highest importance in the professional skills matrix?

A. Holding

B. Plating

C. Production speed and accuracy

D. Receiving

8 These are all highly important tasks to master to become a manager. Which one can cause the greatest monetary loss if *not* handled properly?

A. Cooking accompaniments

B. Reheating food

C. Research

D. Storing food

Notes

Field Project

Real-World Food Production

Introduction

This field project is designed to provide you with an opportunity to learn from practitioners in the restaurant and foodservice industry about what they do to maintain quality in a hectic kitchen.

How different is it to actually work in a foodservice establishment from what you are learning in class? You have been learning about quality standards in food production in an ideal setting, with the time to carry out each assignment sequentially. In the real world, though, unpredictable things happen that must be addressed immediately. The rush of a busy mealtime is a challenge to all the knowledge and skills of a professional: split-second timing is critical.

Assignment

Interview an executive chef or a restaurant or foodservice manager about quality food production. Find out how this professional handles quality in all aspects of the job, as well as how he or she encourages the staff to do it.

Use the following checkpoints to help you plan the interview.

1 Plan the interview.

- ☐ Identify a chef or manager to interview. Ask your instructor for suggestions, if needed.

- ☐ Make arrangements to meet with the interviewee. Call to make an appointment. Explain that you will be interviewing him or her for the class.

- ☐ Prepare the questions that you will ask.

2 Research the establishment.

- ☐ Talk with people who are familiar with the establishment. Read reviews in the local newspapers. If the establishment is a large chain, find out as much as you can about it. Use the Internet whenever possible.

- ☐ What is the establishment's food specialty, theme, or concept?

- ☐ What is the price range?

- ☐ Is the establishment part of a chain or a stand-alone place? If in a chain, is it local or national?

3 Conduct the interview.

- ☐ Find out the establishment's operations.

  - — What is the mission and vision?

  - — Does the establishment have a quality statement? Define what the operation means by quality.

  - — Include a description of the establishment's operation, including its concept.

continued on next page

Real-World Food Production *continued from previous page*

☐ Ask for a tour. Describe the layout, equipment, and staffing. Include the seating capacity of the establishment.

☐ What does the establishment do to define and implement quality?

— View the standardized recipes, specification sheets, menu descriptions, and preparation sheets, if possible.

— Does the interviewee use a problem-solving process to track product deviations?

— Does the operation regularly evaluate product quality? How does the staff do it?

☐ How does the establishment maintain quality in the flow of food?

— Receiving practices

— Storage considerations

— Inventory control, including type of inventory

— Handling fresh produce

☐ What is their use of convenience products?

— How are holding, cooling, and heating food handled? What do they do differently for special events, such as banquets and buffets?

☐ How does the establishment handle special events?

☐ What are the time restraints and service issues for special events?

☐ View the BEO, if possible.

☐ What are quality controls for each event?

☐ What are the differences between banquets and buffets?

☐ Find out about how the manager works with the professional food staff.

☐ How is the professional food staff evaluated and promoted?

☐ What is the professional development for the professional staff?

☐ To what professional associations does the interviewee belong?

Note: *Some of the checkpoints in this assignment suggest viewing forms that a restaurant or foodservice establishment uses. Be aware that some forms may be proprietary and the interviewee may not allow you to see them—or only allow you to see them and not to make copies.*

4 Prepare your report.

☐ Summarize your interview and the results of your meeting.

☐ Your report should be in the form of a narrative describing your interview and meeting. While there are no absolute answers and your observations will be subjective, the report should be thorough and include all requested information as in the checkpoints listed above. Be sure that any conclusions are supported.

Index

Index